Make Sushi at Home

Delicious and Easy Recipes for All Occasions

Hatsue Shigenobu

∷ Contents

＊Measurement unit for this book is 1 cup = 200 ml, 1 table spoon (abbreviation: Tbs.) = 15 ml, and 1 tea spoon (abbr: Ts.) = 5 ml. Adjust the amount appropriately depending on your convenience and preference.
＊The heating time of the microwave shows 600w as the standard. Adjust the temperature depending on your convenience and preference.

▪▪ Introduction

Sushi is the soul food for the Japanese. Sushi culture, based on the necessity of food preservation, is now widely known in a global market as the representative recipe among the many other Japanese cooking. You must have seen as many sushi restaurants not only in Asia but France and the United States. You can even buy colorful sushi finger foods, locally made, in the most of the super markets in the world these days.

In my childhood sushi was the main event menu for my family. When anything to celebrate happened, my mother or grandmother served the sushi in the bowl (*chirashi zushi*) with full of boiled *shiitake* mushrooms in the sweetened soy. It was a fond memory for my brother and me when we were still kids, that my late father joined to our playing store, acting like a professional sushi chef. He lined up almost all of the major sushi ingredients on our kitchen table and got ready for our calls. When we called up our order such as "Excuse me, I want salmon roe sushi next!" or "Please give me thick sushi rolls (*futomaki*) now", he proudly claimed "Certainly!" and made his home-made sushi.

I am still enjoying the sushi gathering in various opportunities. Preparing as many ingredients as possible, I invite people to my hand-roll sushi (*temaki zushi*). Or I cook as many layers of the fried *tofu* as I can, so I can pile up the tower of *tofu* pouches on the table. When someone invited me to their parties, I bring my share of *gimbap*, the sushi rolls with sesame oil-coated seaweed, which I learned in Korea. The fresh and purely white gingers in seasons always make me excited to think of its sweet and sour pickles. Sushi is one of the essential items for our daily cooking life.

Though hand-shaped sushi (*nigiri zushi*) in the authentic style is not easy to challenge, anyone can try sushi recipe to be rolled, mixed, pressed, or wrapped. Sushi has so many variations and adds interesting touches to our dining. In this book, I will show you the very standard recipe that I have repeatedly had since my childhood days, as well as the unique sushi of the local Japanese towns, or the sushi in the playful and nouveau style which is easy to make for the very beginners. Don't be influenced by preconceptions of sushi being too difficult. Turn on the pages and try one of the recipes your eyes happen to pin down. I am confident you will enjoy cooking sushi, not for just eating, but feeling happy when you use your own hands. That is the most attractive point in this soul food, sushi.

Hatsue Shigenobu

▪ The Variations of Sushi Methods in This Book

Sushi is known for having many variations. In this book, I am showing some of the recipes that you can casually try and make successful dishes in your kitchen.

Sushi Rolls

It is the type of the sushi to roll the ingredients with sushi rice. Using the bamboo rolling mat (*makisu*) is essential. Variations of the rolling skin include the seaweed (*nori*) for thick and thin sushi rolls, as well as the pickles or cling films.

Left to right
Seven Fortune Rolls (page 22)
Thin Sushi Rolls (page 34)

Pressed Sushi

Pressed sushi is made by pressing the sushi rice and ingredients onto the sushi molds. The wooden material has been the chief tool for a long time, but you can use other types in various shapes, such as pudding mold dies or cake pans.

Left to right
Sushi in Flan Style (page 58)
Round Cake Sushi (page 62)

Wrapped Sushi

It is the type of sushi to wrap the sushi rice mixed the ingredients with egg omelets, thin slice of meats, or pickles. Wrapping the sushi rice and individual ingredients with the leaves of trees is another way to go.

Left to right
Tiny Sushi Balls (page 68)
Leaf Mustard Wrapped Sushi (page 79)

Pouched Sushi

The most representative type is *tofu* pouch. It is to press the sushi rice into the skin of the fried *tofu* which is shimmered with a lot of sugar and salt. Using the toasted skin as a stuffing material is one of the variations.

Left to right
Tofu Pouches (page 82)
Baked Tofu Pouches (page 84)

Sushi in the Bowl (Mixing ingredients)

It is the type of sushi to mix or scatter the ingredients into sushi rice. Ingredients vary such as seafood, meats, vegetables, eggs, or cooked dry foods and so on. It is essential to use the ingredients originated in Japan, but the western material is occasionally employed as well.

Left to right
Sushi in the Bowl (page 88)
Vegetarian Sushi in the Bowl (page 92)

Sushi in the Bowl (Topping ingredients)

Topping the ingredients on the surface of sushi rice falls into this category. You may enjoy the dish as initially served, or blend the ingredients in the rice yourself. Occasionally this type can have components consisted of the topping and the sushi rice with mixed ingredients.

Left to right
Pickled Sea Bream and Chrysanthemum Petals Sushi in the Bowl (page 96)
Curry and Minced Meat Sushi in the Bowl (page 102)

Steamed Sushi

It is the hot sushi by putting sushi rice in the container, topping ingredients on the rice, and adding the heat with the steamer. Leaf vegetables should not use due to the heating process, so the ingredients are limited to something still tasty after warming up.

Left to right
Steamed Conger Eel Sushi, Osaka Style (page 106)
Steamed Vegetarian and Brown Rice Sushi (page 112)

❖ Essential Tools and Molds

Here introduced on this page is the traditional and indispensable tools for sushi making in the Japanese families. You can replace them with other alternatives when necessary. But a good selection of the tools raises your motivation and skills.

Rice-cooking tub (handai) and Rice paddle (shamoji)

Rice-cooking tub is the wooden bowl with low sides for making and mixing sushi rice and ingredients. *Sawara* cypress is the most common material as it has a function to adjust the heat and humidity of the rice to increase its tastiness. The bowl is also useful to use as a serving dish on the table. Rice paddle is the tool to stir and separate the grains of the rice or sushi rice. Like the rice-cooking tub, the wooden material is recommended. Both devices require giving a slight moisture with vinegar water before use.

Fan (uchiwa)

Fan is the traditional tool for cooling the sushi rice. Sending the wind with a fan to sushi rice makes to blow away the extra moisture or sharp odor of vinegar, and adds the glaze to the skin of the rice.

Washcloth (tenugui)

Washcloth is useful to cover the rice in the rice-cooking tub to prevent it from the dry. It has the air permeability and is quick to dry. Moisturizing it with water and wring it hard dry is the standard way to use. It is multi-functional in many ways, such as to wipe the knives and rice-cooking tub or wrap the lid of the steamer.

Bamboo rolling mat (makisu)

Bamboo rolling mat is made of thin strips of bamboo woven with cotton string. It is the essential tool to create any types of the sushi rolls. This rolling mat is also useful to organize the shape of the thin sushi rolls and the thick omelets, or to dehydrate the wetness of the boiled green vegetables.

Square vat

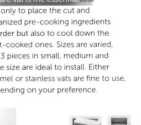

Square vat is the essential tool not only to place the cut and organized pre-cooking ingredients in order but also to cool down the post-cooked ones. Sizes are varied, but 3 pieces in small, medium and large size are ideal to install. Either enamel or stainless vats are fine to use, depending on your preference.

Cling film is a handy tool to use together with the bamboo rolling mat as the layer of the rolled sushi. It is also useful to prevent the sushi rice from sticking to the sushi molds or to organize the proper shape of the wrapped sushi. Cover the prepared and assorted ingredients with the cling film, so they are not dried up.

Cling film

Steamer

Steamer is the utensil to make the steamed sushi. You can choose your favorite material such as stainless steel, or pick up steaming baskets made of bamboo or wood in either Chinese or Japanese style.
Close the lid to steam for any of the types when cooking.

Sushi mold

Sushi mold is the tool for making pressed sushi. The traditional type is made of wood, and in three sizes, depending on the kind of the pressed sushi you want to create. In this book, I am trying to use the alternative tools such as the ones for the terrine, round cake, flan, and round and cube types.

■ Sushi Rice

Ingredients

680 g/23.98 oz. sushi rice

6–8 cm/2.36–3.14 in.
   dried kelp (*konbu*)

Blended Vinegar

50 ml vinegar

1¹/₂ Tbs. sugar

1 Ts. salt

Wash rice and drain water in the sieve. Leave it for 30 minutes. Put the rice in the rice cooker and add water to the required cup measurement (2 cups in this case) marked on inside of the bowl in the rice cooker. Swipe a piece of the dried kelp lightly with the wet washcloth and place it on the rice. Close the lid and switch to cook.

When you want to use the pot for cooking rice ...

Put the rice in the pot and add 360 ml of water. Close the lid, put the pot on the heating table and turn the heat to medium to medium high. See whether the rice starts to get boiled, increase the heating temperature to maximum for 12 minutes. Adjust the heat back to the medium high for another 20–30 minutes, so the moisture of the rice blows away. Stop cooking and allow boiled rice to settle for the next 10 minutes.

Your very first step begins with learning how to make sushi rice.

When it is properly done, you are as good as complete in making sushi.

The method in this spread can be applied to all kinds of recipes in this book.

2

Prepare for the blended vinegar. Pour the vinegar into the bowl and add sugar and salt.

3

Stir the vinegar well with the spoon or other utensils until the sugar and salt dissolve.

4

Blended vinegar is complete. The amount shown here is for the 680 g/23.98 oz. of the rice.

5

Once #1 is ready, remove the kelp and empty the rice to the rice-cooking tub at once.

6

Once the rice is in the rice-cooking tub, distribute the blended vinegar evenly in #4 at once and mix them together. You should use the rice paddle as if it slices through the rice.

7

Turn over the rice with the rice paddle. Do not knead the rice. Otherwise, its texture is spoiled to get soggy.

When the whole amount of the rice is evenly mixed, use the fan to cool down and add glaze to the cooked rice.

9

Wet the washcloth, squeeze it tightly, and spread it over on the rice-cooking tub.

10

Keep covering the washcloth, so the cooked rice is not dried up until you proceed to the next steps of making sushi dishes.

Variations of the blended vinegar

Rice vinegar is the primary material by all means, but you can apply different acid depending on the types of the sushi ingredients. Use your imagination.

a

b

c

d

e

a. Squeezed juice of citron: to add the citron scent or milder sourness to your sushi recipe.

b. Plum vinegar: to add a slight pinkish tint, clean taste, or the plum scent.

c. Balsamic vinegar: when you combine the western ingredients in the recipe, or to add mellowness and body.

d. Lemon: to add the lemon scent or produce the refreshing touch. Grating the lemon skins (organic products are preferable) is a good idea to accommodate the same effect.

e. Dipping sauce of pickled ginger: to add a slight flavor of the ginger.

◈ Omelets

The color and taste of the various omelets are indispensable for sushi recipe.
Here in this spread, I am showing the most common 4 types of the methods commonly
mentioned in this book. All 4 variations intend to enjoy the sweetness to the right extent.

Thin Omelets

Ingredients (for 3 pieces when using
 the frying pan in 24 cm/9.44 in.)

2 pieces egg

1 Ts. potato starch

1 Ts. sugar

A pinch of salt

1 Ts. water

Appropriate amount of salad oil

✳Use the square omelet pan for the thin
omelet for the hand-wrapped sushi rolls.
✳Use the frying pan at 22 cm/8.66 inches in
size for the thin omelet for sushi balls in egg
layer. The height of the thin omelet for sushi
balls should be slightly thicker than the one for
the hand-wrapped sushi balls.

1. Put the potato starch, sugar, salt, and the water in the ingredients into the bowl. Stir and mix well.

2. Crack and drop eggs into the same bowl. Stir and mix further.

3. Filter the eggs with the cooking strainer.

4. Heat the frying pan over medium flame. Shimmer the salad oil on the paper towels, and apply the oil lightly on the surface. Stir #3 once again, so the potato starch is evenly re-distributed.

5. Pour approximately $^1/_3$ amount of eggs onto the frying pan in #4, and spread it over as the thin layer.

6. Bake the egg layer in the low flame for about 1–2 minutes. Use the bamboo sticks to float the edge.

7. Hold the edges with both hands, turn the egg layer upside down. Bake it then for 5 more seconds.

8. Wet the paper towel or washcloth, squeeze tightly and place it over on the vat. Drop the egg layer on the surface of the vat and spread it evenly. Repeat #5 to #8 for 2 more rounds.

Julienned Strip of Thin Omelets

Ingredients (for 3 pieces when
 using the grill pan in 24 cm/9.44 in.)

3 pieces of thin omelet
 made as above

1. Place the thin omelets on the cutting board and cut into 3 vertically even pieces.

2. Turn omelets in #1 at 90 degrees, pile the cut pieces, and straight cut them all.

The Basics of Home-made Sushi

Fine-scrambled Egg

Ingredients (for 2 pieces of eggs)

2 pieces egg

1 Ts. sugar

A pinch of salt

1	2	3	4	5	6

1 Crack and drop eggs into the bowl. Add sugar and salt. Stir and mix well.

2 Pour the whole amount of eggs in #1 onto the fluorine coated frying pan. Heat the frying pan on low flame. Stir the eggs over all with chopsticks for 30 seconds.

3 Turn off the heat and move the frying pan on the table. Stir the eggs with the rubber spatula so that heat percolates evenly.

4 Turn on the heat and return the frying pan on the low flame. Keep stirring the eggs with the chopsticks and keep them soft-boiled.

5 Put down the frying pan from the heat table once again, stir the eggs with the rubber spatula so that the heat percolates evenly.

6 Put on the frying pan on the heat once again, stir with the chopsticks until they turn out to be a fine and moisture scrambled eggs.

Thick Omelets

Ingredients (for 4 pieces of eggs)

4 pieces egg

2$\frac{1}{2}$ Tbs. sugar

A pinch of salt

Appropriate amount of salad oil

1	2	3	4

1 Break the egg shells and drop the whole eggs into the same bowl. Add sugar and salt.

2 Slice and stir well the eggs with the chopsticks.

3 Heat the omelet pan in medium flame. Pour approximately $\frac{1}{3}$ of #2 in the pan, and stir it in a large circle.

4 Once the egg layer is done to look a little more than half-cooked, fold it into the 3 pieces from the far side to the front.

5	6	7	8	9	10

5 Slide the folded eggs to the far side, apply the salad oil thinly on the surface of the pan, Pour another $\frac{1}{3}$ amount of the eggs there.

6 Float the folded eggs with the chopsticks, and let the egg liquid spread underneath of the folded parts.

7 When the new layer of the eggs is done to look a little more than half-cooked, fold it into the 3 pieces from the far side to the front.

8 Repeat the #3 to #7 for the last portion of the eggs.

9 Move the thick omelet on the bamboo rolling mat while it is still hot.

10 Wrap the omelet with the bamboo rolling mat and organize its shape properly. When it is cold enough, cut it into pieces.

Boil Down Dry Foods

Classic sushi recipes such as thick sushi rolls, sushi balls in egg layer with tea-cloth style, or vegetarian sushi in the bowl will not be complete if the dry foods boiled down are missing in their ingredients. Matching them with the sushi rice helps to develop the richness of the taste.

Dried Shiitake Mushrooms

Ingredients (at the amount of your choice)

4 pieces (approximately 24 g/0.84 oz.) dried *shiitake* mushroom

100 ml liquid reconstituted from the dried *shiitake* mushroom

1 Tbs. *sake*

1 Tbs. soy sauce

1 Tbs. sugar

1 Wash dried *shiitake* mushrooms lightly and put it in the Ziploc bag together with 1 cup of water (not listed in the ingredients).

2 Seal the closure of the bag tightly and keep it overnight in the refrigerator.

3 *Shiitake* mushrooms swell after soaking water. Separate mushrooms and reconstituted liquid respectively.

4 Measure to secure 100 ml from the liquid.

   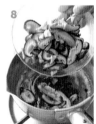

5 Separate the caps and stems of the mushroom. Slice the caps vertically into thin strips.

6 Remove the hard part of the cap and slice it into thin strips.

7 Put the reconstituted liquid, *sake*, soy sauce, sugar in the pan and boil up.

8 Add ingredients in #5 and cook over on a medium flame for 6–7 minutes letting the liquid reduce in the end.

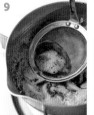 

9 Keep mixing the ingredients and skim off the scum.

10 Boil them over a high flame for another 1–2 minutes until the liquid has nearly evaporated.

Dried Gourds

Ingredients (at the amount of your choice)

20 g/0.70 oz. dried gourd

$^1/_2$ Ts. salt

100 ml soup stock (*dashi*)

2 Tbs. sugar

$1^1/_2$ Tbs. soy sauce

1 Tbs. sweetened *sake* (*mirin*)

1 Cut the edges of the dried gourds at the length matching to the bamboo roll mat. Kitchen scissors are handy to use.

2 Put the dried gourds, add a plenty of water in the bowl, rub them with your hand until they get soft.

3 Squeeze the gourds to dry and move it to another bowl. Sprinkle the salt into the gourds.

4 Rub them with your hand once again until they get soft over all. Rinse the gourds with water and squeeze it to dry.

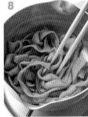

5 Boil the water in the pot, put the ingredients in #4, and scoop them into the colander when they are boiled down.

6 Wash the pot and put the soup stock, sugar, soy sauce, and sweetened *sake*. When the ingredients boil down, put the gourds.

7 Stir the ingredients time to time while heating over the medium flame for 10 minutes.

8 Boil them over a high flame for another 2 minutes until the liquid has nearly evaporated. Turn off the heat and cool it down.

Freeze-dried Tofu

Ingredients (at the amount of your choice)

4 pieces freeze-dried *tofu* (*koya tofu*)

150 ml soup stock

2 Tbs. sweetened *sake*

2 Tbs. sugar

$1^1/_2$ Tbs. soy sauce

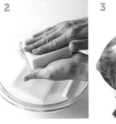

1 Shimmer the freeze-dried *tofu* in the plenty amount of water and reconstitute it until it gets soft.

2 Sandwich the *tofu* between the both of your palms. Repeat this process by changing the water for a few more times.

3 Put the soup stock, soy sauce, sweetened *sake*, sugar in the pot and boil over the maximum flame. When the liquid get boiled, place the *tofu*.

4 Cook the *tofu* over a medium to low flame for 10 minutes.

5 Remove the pan from the heat and let the *tofu* absorb the remaining liquid completely.

◼ Boil Shrimps and Green Vegetables

Orange boiled shrimps add an accent of color to sushi.

Snow peas and green beans that turn bright green when boiled are called *aomi* (green vegetables for garnishing). It is amazing how a pinch of *aomi* changes the prepared dish and makes it look more delicious.

Shrimps

Ingredients (for 4 pieces)

4 pieces shrimp with no heads but shells in medium size

When you plan to cook the shrimps to tempura or deep-fry: Add 3–4 strokes of the hidden cuts on the ventral side of the shrimps. This way their bodies keep straight lines after deep-frying.

1	2	3	4	5
Pierce the bamboo stick between the frontal and ventral joints. Remove the guts.	Pierce the bamboo stick in the middle of the shrimp's tail through to the head to keep its body straight.	Boil the water in the pan and add a pinch of salt and vinegar (not listed in the ingredients). Add the shrimps in the pan and boil for 1–2 minutes.	Remove the bamboo sticks from the body (it is hard to pull them out when the boiled water gets cold) and peel the shells. Remove tails when necessary.	Put the knife edge on the ventral side of the shrimp's body to open.

When you plan to cook the shucked shrimps: Stir the boiled water with chopsticks. This way the body of the shrimps keep round and neat shapes.

Snow Peas, Green Beans

Ingredients (at the amount of your choice)

8 pieces snow pea

50 g/1.76 oz. green bean

1	2	3	4	5
Remove the stem end and string from the snow peas.	Boil the water in the pan and add a pinch of salt (not listed in the ingredients). Salt contributes to keeping the snow peas in refreshing green color.	Add the snow peas to the pan and stir them with chopsticks time to time. Cook them for 30 seconds until the color turns out to be bright green.	Dip the snow pea into the cold water with ice cubes. Pick them up immediately and put them in the colander. Wipe off the moisture.	Cut off the stems of the green beans and boil them for 1 minute. The rest of the process is the same as the snow pea.

▓ Pickle in Sweetened Vinegar

Lotus root and *myoga* are something you should not miss out as the ingredients for the pickles in sweetened vinegar. It is a good idea to keep stocks using these items as they are handy in mixing in the sushi rice, topping on, or using as the decoration.

Lotus Root Cut into Decorative Pieces

Ingredients (at the amount of your choice)

80 g/2.82 oz. lotus root

Sweetened Vinegar

50 ml vinegar

2 Tbs. water

2 Tbs. sugar

$1/4$ Ts. salt

Peel the skin of the lotus root, and make a shallow cut in-between the lotus holes.

Make the cut in along the shapes of the holes and against the cut in spaces. Repeat this process on the other side of the lotus body.

Keep applying #2 process on the whole body of the lotus, so it creates the flower shape.

Make a thin slice at the thickness of 2–3 mm/0.07–0.11 in. and soak the sliced pieces in the water.

Boil the water in the pan and put #4 in.

Keep boiling it for 1 minute until its color becomes translucent.

Pour the sweetened vinegar ingredients in the bowl and mix. Drain the water from #6, add it to the sweetened vinegar, and cool it down.

Myoga

Ingredients (at the amount of your choice)

6 pieces *myoga*

Sweetened Vinegar

150 ml vinegar

$2^1/2$ Tbs. sugar

$1/3$ Ts. salt

Cut *myoga* vertically into half.

Boil the water and dip #1 in quickly.

Put *myoga* in the colander immediately.

Place the sweetened vinegar ingredients in the bowl and mix. Add #3 while it is still hot. Cool it down.

■■ *Pickled Gingers* *Gari*

Pickled gingers, or *gari*, are the thin ginger slices pickled in the sweetened vinegar and are something you would always want to add to your sushi dishes. If you use the fresh gingers for this recipe, you can retain the pale pink pickled liquid due to the action of the vinegar. When using the standard ginger, the color of the pickled liquid is not noticeable.

New Gingers

Ingredients (at the amount of your choice)

150 g/5.29 oz. new ginger

Sweetened Vinegar

150 ml vinegar

$2^1/_2$ Tbs. sugar

$1/_3$ Ts. salt

1

Make thin slices of the fresh ginger with the slicer. If you don't own the slicer, you can use your knives to obtain the similar result.

2

Put the sweetened vinegar ingredients in the bowl.

3

Stir well and let the sugar and salt dissolve well.

4

Boil the water in the pan, put #1 in the colander, and place it into the boiled water.

5

Stir the ginger lightly in the colander for 5 seconds and remove it from the heat.

6

Drain the water and pour the sliced new gingers into the sweetened vinegar.

7

Cool down the sliced gingers. When you preserve the finished ones, make sure to keep soaking them in the sweetened vinegar.

The Basics of Home-made Sushi

Gingers

Ingredients (at the amount of your choice)

150 g/5.29 oz. standard ginger

Sweetened Vinegar

150 ml vinegar

$2^1/_2$ Tbs. sugar

$^1/_3$ Ts. salt

Shake off the skin using the edge of the spoon, or with the similar utensils. Make thin slices of the ginger with the slicer. Prepare for the sweetened vinegar ingredients in the bowl.

Boil the water in the pan, put #1 and boil it for 15 seconds or so.

Pour the cooked ginger into the colander and drain the water well.

Pour the sliced gingers into the sweetened vinegar.

Cool down the sliced gingers. When you preserve the finished ones, make sure to keep soaking them in the sweetened vinegar.

Hajikami Gingers

Hajikami ginger is made from the roots with the fresh leaves (it is also called *Yanaka Shoga*).
When this root is pickled in the sweetened vinegar, the pickled liquid turns out to be in pretty pink color, matching perfectly to sushi or garnishes to the seafood cooking. Let's try this recipe, as the ingredients and amount of the sweetened vinegar are the same as the above.

Pick up 6–10 pieces of *Yanaka Shoga*. Leave 6–8 cm/2.36–3.15 in. of the green stems and chop off the leaves.

Cut out the root bulbs per stems and wash them in the water.

Slice the edge of the ginger roots a little and organize the shapes appropriately. Keep the sliced side of the ginger roots as well.

Boil the water in the pan, put #3 as well as the sliced edge, and pick them up from the boiled water immediately.

Drain the water and put the gingers into the sweetened vinegar while they are still hot.

Leave the gingers in the sweetened vinegar until they absorb seasonings.

▪ Variations of Garnishes *Yakumi and Tsumamono*

Pickled Gingers

Made from the new and the standard gingers (see pages 16 & 17).

Hajikami Gingers

Gingers with leaves, pickled in the sweetened vinegar (see page 17).

Japanese Horseradish

The raw *wasabi*. Mainly used by scraping skin and grating or cutting into strips.

Flower of the Green Perilla

Mainly treated by drawing the flower through your hands to drop to the *sashimi* soy sauce.

Benitade

A variation of the marshpepper knotweed, known with its spicy taste and amaranth color.

Young Buds of Japanese Pepper

Sansho. One of the most representative kinds for the Japanese potherb.

Green Perilla

Cut into strips to enjoy its fresh scent.

Myoga

Handy to mix with the sushi rice when finely chopped.

Spring Onion

Handy to mix with sushi rice, or scatter on it when finely chopped. May be replaced with the versatile leek.

Welsh Onion

Best use when fincly chopped. The another one of the most representative variations as the Japanese potherb. Mainly in use of the white stem parts.

Fruits of Japanese Pepper

Commonly known for its use boiled down in soy.

Kneaded Wasabi

Convenient to use as the alternatives of the raw *wasabi*. Convenient when you need only a little amount.

Citron Pepper Condiment

Made from the pepper and the citron skin, the refreshing and spicy taste of citron pepper condiment is characteristic.

Kneaded Plum Meat

Tastes vary according to the manufacturers or brands.

Pickled Plum

Remove the seed, chop the flesh to use.

Garnishes in the sushi recipe have many varieties.

Condiment (*yakumi*) brings out the taste of the main dishes with a little amount while trimmings (*tsumamono*) that add the colors and scents.

Here in this spread, I will show you some of those selections.

Crispy Plum

Known for its crispy texture. The photo above shows its small fruits to slice.

Strip of Citron Skin

Fine strip that is peeled from the citron skin. Only the yellow surface is in use.

Sliced Citron Skin

Good to mix with the sushi rice. Grating type is also a good match.

Powdered Red Perilla

Known for its refreshing scent and a good companion to the freshly cooked rice.

Powdered Green Laver

Dried and powdered green laver or sea lettuce.

White Sesame

The good scent when roasted or grated.

Black Sesame

The good scent when roasted or grated. More robust than its white variation.

Parsley

One of the representative variations of the western herbs in the Japanese cooking. Useful to add the color and scent when finely chopped.

Pickled Caper

The bud is used for the vinegared or salted.

Mustard into a Paste

Milder pungent taste than the standard type.

Grain Mustard

Little pungent taste in general, but focused on the sour and the savory.

Pink Pepper

Dried fruit of the Peruvian pepper. Good to add color on your sushi recipe.

Paprika Powder

Little pungent taste, though its red color reminds it. Only a small amount is enough to use to add some color.

Curry Powder

Made by blending a few kinds of the spices. Good when you want some accent on your dish.

Gochujang

Korean *miso* with chili pepper which contains spicy, flavor, and sweetness.

Sushi Rolls Maki Zushi

Preparing for the ingredients and sushi rice, rolling each piece with seaweed,
you might think that making sushi rolls is a time-consuming task.
But making it is an entertainment event and I am sure you will have a fun time
to tackle it. The thick sushi rolls with many kinds of the ingredients stuffed,
the thin sushi rolls at one-bite size, the variations of thin sushi rolls,
and the hand-wrapped sushi rolls in any combination with your fingers. . .
all are delicious when filling your mouth.

⠵ *Seven Fortune Rolls* *Shichifuku Eho Maki*

It is the tradition in Japan to eat this roll on the day before the calendrical beginning of spring, facing the lucky direction of the year. Seven Fortune Rolls are supposed to bite into the whole piece without cutting. I am using the shrimps or prawns (lucky symbol too) to cook as *tempura* and roll them along with the seven ingredients. A little fiesta to welcome spring.

Ingredients (for 2 rolls)

4 pieces shrimp or prawn
  (headless, with shells)

Tempura **Batter**

 2 Tbs. *tempura* flour

 2 Tbs. water

Appropriate amount of frying oil

2 pieces cucumber diced at
  7–8mm/0.27–0.31 in.

$1/4$ pack white radish sprout

6 pieces green perilla

20 g/0.70 oz. *shibazuke*
  (chopped and pickled vegetables
  with the red perilla leaves)

1 Tbs. flying fish roe

20 g/0.70 oz. butterbur stalks
  (boiled in soy sauce, or *kyarabuki*)

340 g/11.99 oz. sushi rice (see page 8)

2 sheets toasted seaweed

1 Remove the shells, tails, and veins of shrimps or prawns. Make 2–3 hidden cuts on the vein side, so that the body keeps straight. Mix the *tempura* ingredients together, dip the shrimps or prawns into it, and deep-fry them at the medium temperature.

2 Cut the stem of the white radish sprouts and green perilla. Mince the *shibazuke*.

3 Place 1 piece of seaweed on the bamboo rolling mat and spread the half amount of sushi rice, leaving approximately 2 cm/0.78 in. of the space at the far end.

4 Place the green perilla on the foreground first, each half amount of cucumbers, *shibazuke*, and butterbur stalks next. Place each half amount of the shrimps or prawns in #1, white radish sprouts, flying fish roe on to the 1st and 2nd batch of the vegetables (see photo a).

5 Roll down the ingredients (see photos b & c) from the foreground, hold hard to organize the shape of the roll (see photo d). Repeat this process for 1 more piece of the roll.

6 Serve the rolls on the plate without cutting and use your fingers to enjoy.

a

b

c

d

Extra Large Rolls

These thick rolls require 1.5 times more of the sushi rice, with 2 pieces of seaweed sheets to connect. Besides the seafood such as salmon or calamari, add omelets, cucumbers, gourds to add a gorgeous touch to your dish. This recipe is as pleased as can be without anything extra.

Ingredients (for 1 roll)

Lean tuna for *sashimi* use, cutting out to sticks at 7–8 mm/0.27–0.31 in. at width x seaweed sheet's width in size

Salmon for *sashimi* use, cutting out to sticks at 7–8 mm/0.27–0.31 in. at width x seaweed sheet's width in size

Kisslip cuttlefish for *sashimi* use, cutting out to sticks at 7–8 mm/0.27–0.31 in. at width x seaweed sheet's width in size

Appropriate amount of thick omelet (see page 11)

¹/₃ bundle Japanese honewort

2–3 pieces picked pokeweed

1 piece cucumber lightly salted pickle

2–3 pieces boil down dry gourd (see page 13)

3 pieces boiled down dry *shiitake* mushroom (see page 12)

510 g/17.98 oz. sushi rice (see page 8)

2 sheets toasted seaweed

1. Cut thick omelets into the sticks at 1 cm/0.39 in. Dip the Japanese honewort into the boiled water, pick it up and throw it into the cold water. Squeeze out the excess water from it.

2. Spread the 2 sheets of seaweed on the bamboo roll mat vertically by overlapping at 3–4 cm/1.18–1.57 in. Spread the sushi rice leaving the space at 5 cm/1.96 in. in the far side.

3. Place cucumbers in the foreground first. Put all other ingredients, making sure that the color of each row not to overlap, as much as possible.

4. Roll down the ingredients (see photo a) from the foreground, hold hard to organize the shape of the roll.

5. Cut the roll into pieces at a width for an easy bite (see photo b). When cutting, wipe the knife with the wet washcloth at a time, which makes easier to keep working.

Seattle Rolls, California Rolls

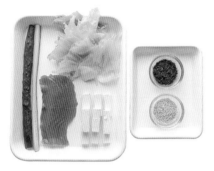

California Rolls

Ingredients (for 1 roll)

5–6 pieces crab-flavored fish paste

$^1/_4$ piece avocado

$^1/_2$ piece cucumber

2 Tbs. flying fish roe

$1^1/_2$ Tbs. mayonnaise

170 g/5.99 oz. sushi rice (see page 8)

1 sheet toasted seaweed

Seattle Rolls

Ingredients (for 1 roll)

4–5 pieces smoked salmon

2 packs (approx. 35 g/1.23 oz.) cream cheese (individual packaging)

2 pieces of cut stick at 7–8 mm square/0.27–0.31 in. in size cucumber

1 piece lettuce leaf

200 g/7.05 oz. sushi rice (see page 8)

2 Tbs. white sesame parched

1 Tbs. powdered green laver

1 sheet toasted seaweed

1. Cut a pack of cream cheese into 3 sticks and tear the lettuce leaf by hands in small batches.
2. Place the cling film a little larger than the size of the seaweed, and then the seaweed on the cling film. Spread the sushi rice over the seaweed. Sprinkle the sesame and powdered green laver.
3. Place the cling film again on #2's surface, hold it lightly and turn it out upside down (see photo a). Remove the cling film on the seaweed.
4. Place the lettuce leaf and cucumber in the foreground, top the smoked salmon and cream cheese and roll it down, making sure not to wrap up the cling film in (see photo b). Hold hard to organize the shape of the roll.
5. Cut the roll into pieces for an easy bite (see photo c) over the cling film. Remove the cling film.

1. Remove the seeds and skins of the avocado, and cut into pieces at 7–8 mm/0.27–0.31 in. at width. Cut the cucumbers into strips.
2. Place the cling film a little larger than the size of the seaweed, and then the seaweed on the cling film. Spread the sushi rice over the seaweed. Place the cling film again on the surface, hold it lightly and turn it out upside down. Remove the cling film on the seaweed.
3. Place the cucumber in the foreground, top the avocado and crab-flavored fish paste, and squeeze the mayonnaise (see photo d).
4. Roll #3 down, making sure not to wrap up the cling film in. Hold hard to organize the shape of the roll. Cut the rolls into pieces at the size of smooth bite over the cling film. Remove the cling film and top the flying fish roe.

Seattle Rolls

California Rolls

Seattle rolls and California rolls became the standard items after re-imported from the US. Seattle rolls have the best combination of smoked salmon, cream cheese, and raw vegetables. The delicious assortment of the crab-flavored fish paste, avocado and mayonnaise will become a habit.

⬛ *Rainbow Rolls* *Tazuna Zushi*

Rainbow rolls have another name, *tazuna zushi* (horse saddle sushi), as its shape looks like the horse saddle. What makes it distinct from other sushi rolls is the way to lay the ingredients. Cut the shrimps, cucumbers, and carrots into thin slices and line up them diagonally. Adding the thin omelet is also a nice touch.

Ingredients (for 2 rolls)

2–3 pieces boiled shrimp (see page 14)

4 pieces cucumber, sliced with peeler

4 pieces carrot, sliced with peeler

2 pieces sliced cheese

340 g/11.99 oz. sushi rice (see page 8)

1 Halve the shrimps vertically. Cut the cucumbers at 5–6 cm/1.96–2.36 in. in size and sprinkle the salt (not listed in the ingredients). Leave it for approx. 5 minutes. Dip the carrots into the boiled water and cut them at 5–6 cm/1.96–2.36 in. in size. Cut the sliced cheese into 3 pieces.

2 Place the cling film on the bamboo rolling mat and put a chopstick for the indication of the straight line. Lay the half amount of each ingredient in the attractive color combination by overlapping a little each other (see photo a).

3 Make the half amount of sushi rice into the ball in half-ecliptic shape, place it vertically in the center of the ingredients. Remove the chopstick.

4 Roll #3 down, making sure not to wrap up the cling film in. Hold hard to organize the shape of the roll (see photo b). Repeat this process for one more roll.

5 Cut the rolls into pieces at the size for an easy bite over the cling film. Remove the cling film.

Chinese Cabbage Pickles Rolls *Hakusaizuke Maki*
Coleseed Green Pickles Rolls *Nozawanazuke Maki*

Chinese Cabbage Pickles Rolls

Ingredients (for 1 roll)

60 g/2.11 oz. Chinese cabbage pickle (select the leaf parts)

1 piece chicken breast strip

30 g/1.05 oz. Chinese yam

1 Tbs. kneaded plum meat

150 g/5.29 oz. sushi rice (see page 8)

1　Boil the chicken breast strips in the hot water with 1 Tbs. of Japanese *sake* (not included in the ingredients) for approx. 5–6 minutes. Make sure for the hot water to cover the meat completely. After the heat disperse to the meat, pick them up on the colander. When the meat is cooled down, strip them with your hands into the bite-size pieces.

2　Peel off the Chinese yam's skin and cut them into the sticks at 5 mm/0.19 in. in size.

3　Spread a few pieces of the Chinese cabbage pickles over the bamboo rolling mats, by changing the top and bottom directions, so the pickles sheet will eventually be the same as the standard seaweed sheet size.

4　Spread the sushi rice leaving the space at 2–3 cm/0.78–1.18 in. on the far side. Place the kneaded plum meat on the foreground, lay #1 and Chinese yams. Roll down the ingredients from the foreground (see photo on the left). Hold it tightly to organize its shape.

5　Cut the roll into pieces at a bite size.

Coleseed Green Pickles Rolls

Ingredients (for 1 roll)

30 g/1.05 oz. coleseed green pickle (select the leaf parts)

Appropriate amount of thick omelet (see page 11)

150 g/5.29 oz. sushi rice (see page 8)

1　Cut the thick omelets into approx. 3 cm/1.18 in. sticks.

2　Spread a few pieces of the coleseed green pickles over the bamboo rolling mat, by changing the top and bottom directions, so the pickles sheet will eventually be the same as the standard seaweed sheet size.

3　Spread the sushi rice leaving the space at 2 cm/0.78 in. on the far side. Place #1 at the far side. Roll down the ingredients from the foreground. Hold it tightly to organize its shape.

4　Cut the roll into the pieces in size for an easy bite.

Both types use the vegetable pickles to roll up the ingredients.
Chinese cabbage pickles rolls include the chicken breast strips, Chinese yams,
and kneaded plum meat, while coleseed green pickles rolls assorts the thick omelets.
All ingredients go perfectly with the rice and so there is no wonder these two sushi rolls
are delicious and ideal to serve at the end of the meals after drinking alcohol drinks.

Coleseed Green Pickles Rolls

Chinese Cabbage Pickles Rolls

▪▪ Gimbap

Gimbap is the Korean roll sushi and is getting popular in Japan. The ingredients include the sweet and hot Korean beef barbecue with sweet soy sauce flavoring, thick omelets, perilla frutescens, Chinese cabbage *kimchi* and so on.

Though it is the roll variation, *gimbap* does not use the sushi rice but the plain type. It is unique in seasoning the rice with the sesame oil and salt.

a

b

Ingredients (for 1 roll)

Korean Beef Barbecue

80 g/2.82 oz. beef trimmings

$^1/_3$ Ts. salad oil

$^2/_3$ Tbs. Korean barbecue sauce

Appropriate amount of thick omelet (see page 11)

Yellow pickled radish

2–3 pieces perilla frutescens leaf (or green perilla)

50 g/1.76 oz. Chinese cabbage kimchi

150 g/5.29 oz. plain rice

For Seasoning Rice

1 Ts. sesame oil

$^1/_3$ Ts. salt

1 sheet toasted seaweed

Appropriate amount of sesame oil

A sprinkling of white sesame parched

1. Make the Korean beef barbecue first. Stir fry the beef with the salad oil for 1–2 minutes, add the Korean barbecue sauce and disperse it in the beef. When the meat is cooled down, drain the liquid a little.

2. Cut the thick omelet into the sticks at 1 cm/0.39 in. in size. Mince the *kimchi* and squeeze the liquid lightly. Halve the leaves of the perilla frutescens vertically.

3. Season the rice with sesame oil and salt.

4. Place the seaweed on the bamboo rolling mat. Spread #3 over the mat leaving the space at 2 cm/0.78 in. at the far side.

5. Line up the leaves of perilla frutescens on the rice, and place the thick omelets, yellow pickled radish, kimchi, and Korean beef barbecue (see photo a). Roll down the ingredients from the foreground,

hold it tightly and organize the shape.

6. Apply the sesame oil on the seaweed (see photo b), sprinkle the white sesame, and cut the roll into pieces in size for an easy bite.

Thin Sushi Rolls *Hosomaki*

The attractiveness in the thin sushi rolls with various ingredients is in its simple and finger-food style. Here in this spread, I am showing the 4 standard recipes.

When you stuff the finished rolls in the square box, its orderly view is quite impressive. Adjust the amount of Japanese horseradish, to taste.

Tuna Rolls *Tekka Maki*
Cucumber Rolls *Kappa Maki*
Gourd Rolls *Kampyo Maki*
Wasabi Rolls

Ingredients (for 2 rolls each)

Tuna Rolls

Lean tuna for *sashimi* use, cutting out to sticks at 7–8 mm/0.27–0.31 in. at width x seaweed sheet's double width in size

140 g/4.93 oz. sushi rice (see page 8)

1 sheet toasted seaweed

Appropriate amount of grated Japanese horseradish

Cucumber Rolls

Cucumber, cutting out to sticks at 7–8 mm/0.27–0.31 in.

140 g/4.93 oz. sushi rice (see page 8)

1 sheet toasted seaweed

Appropriate amount of grated Japanese horseradish

Gourd Rolls

Boiled gourd (see page 13)

140 g/4.93 oz. sushi rice (see page 8)

1 sheet toasted seaweed

Wasabi Rolls

20 g/0.70 oz. Japanese horseradish, cutting into strips

140 g/4.93 oz. sushi rice (see page 8)

1 sheet toasted seaweed

Appropriate amount of pickled ginger (see page 17)

1 Make tuna rolls. Halve the seaweed sheet, place it horizontally on the bamboo rolling mat, and spread the half amount of sushi rice leaving the space at 1 cm/0.39 in. on the far side.

2 Apply the Japanese horseradish on the foreground. Place 1 piece of lean tuna first (see photo a) and roll down the ingredients from the foreground, hold hard to organize the shape of the roll (see photo b). Repeat this process one more time to make another roll.

3 Repeat #1 and #2 to make the cucumber rolls.

4 Repeat #1 and #2 to make the gourd and *wasabi* rolls but without applying the Japanese horseradish.

5 Cut the roll into pieces at a 3 cm/1.18 in. width for an easy bite. Add pickled gingers to assort.

Wasabi Rolls   Gourd Rolls   Cucumber Rolls   Tuna Rolls

Thin Sushi Rolls: Variation *Kawari Hosomaki*

Triangle Rolls

Square Rolls

Teardrop Rolls

a

b

c

Triangle Rolls
Square Rolls
Teardrop Rolls

Ingredients (for 1 roll each for the triangle and square rolls. For the teardrop rolls, 2 rolls.)

Triangle Rolls

1–2 pieces coleseed green pickle (stem parts)

100 g/3.52 oz. sushi rice (see page 8)

1/2 sheet toasted seaweed

2 Tbs. black sesame parched

Square Rolls

3–4 pieces crab-flavored fish paste

100 g/3.52 oz. sushi rice (see page 8)

1/2 sheet toasted seaweed

Appropriate amount of shredded kelp

Teardrop Rolls

200 g/7.05 oz. sushi rice (see page 8)

1 Ts. each dried red perilla and powdered green laver

1 sheet toasted seaweed

1. Make the triangle rolls. Cut the coleseed green pickles into pieces matching to the length of the seaweed.

2. Place the cling film a little larger than the size of the seaweed, and then the seaweed on the cling film. Spread the sushi rice over the seaweed. Place the cling film again on the surface, hold it lightly and turn it out upside down. Remove the cling film on the seaweed. Place the coleseed green pickles in the foreground and roll it down, making sure not to wrap up the cling film in.

3. Use the bamboo rolling mat and scraper (or other utensils) to organize the triangle shape of the rolls (see photo a), remove the cling film, and cover the rolls with sesame over all. Cut the rolls into pieces in size for an easy bite.

4. Make the square rolls. Place the cling film a little larger than the size of the seaweed, and then the seaweed on the cling film. Spread the sushi rice over the seaweed. Place the cling film again on the surface, hold it lightly and turn it out upside down. Remove the cling film on the seaweed. Place

the crab-flavored fish paste in the foreground and roll it down, making sure not to wrap up the cling film in.

5. Use the bamboo rolling mat and scraper (or other utensils) to organize the square shape of the rolls (see photo b), remove the cling film, and cover the rolls with the shredded kelp over all. Cut the rolls into pieces at the size of the smooth bite.

6. Make the teardrop rolls. Split the sushi rice in half, and mix the each portion with the dried red perilla and powdered green laver respectively.

7. Spread the half size of the seaweed sheet over the bamboo rolling mat and place the rice with the red perilla evenly. Roll it down from the foreground, and crush the far side of the mat with fingers to sharpen the edge of the teardrop shape (see photo c). Repeat this process with the rice with powdered green and cut them into pieces for an easy bite. Make the two variations of the teardrop sushi rolls alternative.

The 3 types of the thin sushi rolls on this spread is the variations from the standard 4 kinds on the previous spread. They are triangle rolls, square rolls, and teardrop rolls. Triangle rolls have another name, *Fuji Zushi*, as they look like the Japanese wisteria flowers (*fuji*) when overlapping and putting together on the dish.
The beautiful shapes of these sushi will give a gorgeous touch to your meal table.

Square Rolls

Teardrop Rolls

Triangle Rolls

✦ *Whirlpool Roll*

Let's try making the whirlpool roll using the sushi rice with the coloring agents for food. Black sesame for the color of black, curry powder for yellow, parsley for green, luncheon meat for pink creates a colorful presentation on your table. There are not much of the real ingredients for this recipe, but the completed dish looks fantastic. You can enjoy the various and different tastes per portions.

Ingredients (for 1 roll)

300 g/10.58 oz. sushi rice (see page 8)

1 Tbs. grated black sesame

$^{1}/_{2}$ Ts. curry powder

1 Tbs. minced parsley

30 g/1.05 oz. minced luncheon meat

1 sheet toasted seaweed

Appropriate amount of pickled ginger (see page 16)

1 Split the sushi rice into the 4 equal portions. Mix the rice with the sesame, parsley, curry powder, and the luncheon meat respectively.

2 Spread the seaweed over the bamboo rolling mat, place the sushi rice with sesame, curry powder, parsley, and the luncheon meat in order on the seaweed, and extend the ingredients by leaving the space at 1–2 cm/0.39–0.78 in. at the far end.

3 Roll down #2 from the foreground, hold it tightly to organize the shape of the roll.

4 Cut the roll into pieces for an easy bite, and add the pickled gingers.

❖ Vietnamese Rice Paper Rolls

This roll in Asian taste uses the Vietnamese rice paper instead of the seaweed sheet. Though there is the sushi rice in the roll, the method to make is the same as the real fresh spring roll. Dip it in the sweet chili sauce and enjoy!

Ingredients (for 4 rolls)

8 pieces boiled shrimp

3 thin slices roast pork

1 piece leaf of red leaf lettuce

4 pieces green perilla

1 bundle coriander

4 sheets Vietnamese rice paper

340 g/11.99 oz. sushi rice (see page 8)

Appropriate amount of sweetened chili sauce

1 Pour a pinch of the vinegar and salt (not listed in the ingredients) into the hot water and boil the shrimps, and drain the water. Slice the roast pork into thin strips. Tear the red leaf lettuce with your hands and cut the corianders into slices at 3–4 cm/1.18–1.57 in. at length.

2 Spread the squeezed wet washcloth. Soak the rice paper in the water, one by one, and place them on the washcloth. Place 2 pieces of the shrimp into the foreground, and then 1 piece of the green perilla with its back side of the leaves on the front. Spread approximately ¼ amount of the whole sushi rice over the green perilla, so that it completely covers.

3 Place approximately ¼ each amount of the whole roast pork, red leaf lettuce, and coriander on the sushi rice. Fold the both edges of the rice paper first and roll down the ingredients, just like you do for the spring roll. Repeat this process 3 times to complete 4 pieces of the rolls. Add the sweetened chili sauce as the accent.

Use the fish sausage as the core of the roll,
and make the finished *nori* rolls with the thin omelet.
The cheese and whole grain mustard give a punch to this recipe.
Though the finished rolls are delicious after it gets cold,
nothing is better than to enjoy while the omelets are still warm.

◾ Nori and Thin Omelet Inside-out Rolls

Ingredients (for 2 rolls)

2 pieces fish sausage

2 Tbs. whole grain mustard

2 packs sliced cheese

340 g/11.99 oz. sushi rice (see page 8)

2 pieces toasted seaweed

1 piece egg

$^1/_3$ Ts. sugar

A pinch of salt

1 Ts. water

A pinch of salad oil

1   Cut the seaweed sheet at the same length as the border of the egg.

2   Place a sheet of the seaweed on the bamboo rolling mat and spread the half portion of the sushi rice by leaving the space at 1–2 cm/0.39–0.78 in. at the far end. Apply the half portion of the whole grain mustard, and put the 1 piece of the sliced cheese on. Place the fish sausage in the foreground, roll it down, hold tightly to organize the shape of the roll. Make one more roll repeating the process as above.

3   Pour the sugar, salt, and the water (indicated about as above), mix them all, and add the egg. Stir further and filter the liquid using the colander.

4   Apply the thin layer of the salad oil on the square omelet pan. Pour the half portion of #3. Spread it over as the thin layer. Before the first piece of the omelet is not dry, pour the rest of the egg liquids to be half-cooked. Slide the folded eggs to the far side, apply the salad oil thinly on the surface of the omelet pan, and pour the half of the rest of the eggs there (see photo). Repeat this process for 1 more roll, and cut the roll into pieces for an easy bite.

Sushi Rolls

Tempura Rolls with Sea Urchin and Nori

Make a luxury *nori* roll sushi with the sea urchin and green perilla as the ingredients, and deep-fry after the *tempura* flours on the body. Put the roll just fried in the mouth while it is still hot, you will then feel that the fragrance of the sea urchin spreading over in your mouth.

Ingredients (for 3 rolls)

30 g/1.05 oz. sea urchin

3 pieces green perilla

170 g/5.99 oz. sushi rice (see page 8)

Tempura Batter

  2 Tbs. *tempura* flour

  2 Tbs. water

  Appropriate amount of frying oil

1 Place the $^1/_2$ size of the seaweed sheet vertically as the long strip on the bamboo rolling mat. Spread the $^1/_3$ amount of the sushi rice leaving the space at 2–3 cm/0.78–1.18 in. on the far side. Place a piece of green perilla on the foreground and $^1/_3$ amount of sea urchin. Roll it down from the front, hold it tightly to organize the shape of the roll. Repeat this process for 2 more rolls.

2 Mix the *tempura* batter ingredients.

3 Pour #1 into #2, deep-fry it with the medium heat (see photo) for approx. 1 minute. Drain the oil and cut into pieces for an easy bite.

◫ Hand-wrapped Sushi Rolls: Variation

The deliciousness in the hand-roll sushi is limitless.

You can try a countless combination of the ingredients from the seafood, meats, and vegetables, to the garnishes like the mayonnaise, citron pepper condiment, and *gochujang*. You can even replace the seaweed to the vegetables to wrap the rolls.

Here in this spread, I have listed up some of the best combinations I tried and can recommend with confidence.

Sea bream and crispy plum with olive oil:

Toasted seaweed + sushi rice + roquette + sea bream *sashimi* + slices of the crispy plum + a dollop of olive oil

Lean tuna, pokeweed, natto trio:

Toasted seaweed + sushi rice + lean tuna *sashimi* + pokeweed pickles + crushed *natto* mixing in the supplement sauce

Luncheon meat and bitter gourd, Okinawan style:

Toasted seaweed + sushi rice + thin slices of the luncheon meat + thin slices of the bitter gourd, salted and lightly boiled + a sprinkle of the bonito flakes

Sweet shrimp and avocado, scented with the coriander:

Toasted seaweed + sushi rice + sweet shrimp *sashimi* + lemon cut into quarter slices + coriander

Cheese, tubular fish-paste, pickled wasabi, seaweed, double-wrapped with seaweed and celtuce:

Celtuce + toasted seaweed + sushi rice cereals + sliced cheese + tubular fish-paste cut into sticks + pickled *wasabi*

Scallop adductor and paprika, flavored with the grain mustard:

Celtuce + sushi rice + grain mustard + thin slices of the scallop adductor + red paprika cut into strips

Raw ham, gouda cheese, pineapple:

Red leaf lettuce + sushi rice + thin slices of raw ham + thin slices of the pineapple + peeled slices of the gouda cheese

Roast pork, mustard plant pickled, and cucumber, Chinese trio:

Red leaf lettuce + rice cereals + thin slices of the roasted pork + cucumber cut into strips + thin slices of the mustard plant pickled

Pork shabu and pickles with red perilla leaves rolled up with the boiled cabbage leaves:

Boiled cabbage leaves (removing the cores) + sushi rice + boiled pork *shabu* + roughly chopped pickles with red perilla leaves + mayonnaise

Salmon, myoga, and miso wrapped with boiled cabbage:

Boiled cabbage (removing the cores) + sushi rice + salmon *sashimi* + *myoga* vertically cut into strips + white radish sprouts + *miso*

Broiled maitake mushroom and canned salmon meat, wrapped with leaves of perilla frutescens:

Leaves of perilla frutescens (or green perilla) + sushi rice + grilled *maitake* mushroom + canned salmon meat marinated with mayonnaise + a sprinkle of the powdered green laver

Deep-fried chicken and leaves of perilla frutescens, topped with gochujang:

Leaves of perilla frutescens (or green perilla) + sushi rice + deep-fried chicken cut into strips + white radish cut into strips + *gochujang*

Flaked meat and sautéed burdock, topped with mayonnaise:

Thin omelet + toasted seaweed + flaked meat[*1] + sautéed burdock + mayonnaise

Sausage and asparagus, double-wrapped with seaweed and thin omelet:

Thin omelet + toasted seaweed + sushi rice + sausage grilled and halved + boiled and halved asparagus + tomato ketchup

Octopus sashimi and red-leaved chicory, seasoned with the lemon and cheese:

Red-leaved chicory + sushi rice + octopus *sashimi* + roughly minced lemon + olive oil + Parmesan cheese

Seared cow and caper wrapped with the red-leaved chicory:

Red-leaved chicory + sushi rice + shredded laver + seared and cut beef into strips[*2] + caper

Crispy pork and radish sprinkled salt and rubbed in, seasoned with citron pepper condiment:

Radish sprinkled salt and rubbed in[*3] + sushi rice + crispy-grilled pork back ribs, cut into strips + versatile leek + citron pepper condiment

Steamed chicken and spicy cod roe wrapped with the radish sprinkled salt and rubbed in:

Radish sprinkled salt and rubbed in + sushi rice grains + steamed chicken stripped by hands[*4] + spicy cod roe + Japanese honewort

＊1 : Recipe of the flaked meat: Fry the 100 g/3.52 oz. of the mixed and ground beef and pork with the salad oil, and season with the 1 Ts. of Worcester sauce and $1/3$ Ts. of soy sauce.

＊2 : Recipe of the seared cow: Season the seared cow meat 200 g/7.05 oz. with $1/3$ Ts. of salt and a sprinkle of the rough-grained black pepper. Apply a thin layer of the salad oil on the hot pan, place the meat, and cool it down.

＊3 : Recipe of the radish sprinkled salt and rubbed in: Cut into thin strips and season the 10 pieces (120 g/4.23 oz.) of the white radish with 1 Tbs. of vinegar, $1/3$ Ts. of salt. Leave it for approx. 15 minutes and squeeze the water out.

＊4 : Recipe for the steamed chicken: Put the 1 piece of chicken breast meat in the pot, along with the 2 Tbs. of *sake* and 100 ml of water. Bring the water to a boil. Once the water is boiled, skim off the scum, close the lid, and steam the meat to disperse.

▪▪ Pressed Sushi   Oshi Zushi

Authentic pressed sushi uses the sushi molds to make a beautiful and
dignified piece of food art. Whatever ingredients you use,
matching them with the sushi rice guarantees the exquisite taste.
The joy to challenge creating the pressed sushi is not limited to its look only.
Just try a different type of molds you can find in your daily life, such as glass,
empty cheese box, as well as the containers for flan, or terrine.
Press, pause, and press again to keep trying to make as many different
types of the sushi pieces as you like.
You will find the immense joy of home-made delicacies.

▦ Sea Bream

The kelp brings out the flavor condensed when pickled with the white fish *sashimi* meat. Here on this page, I will show you the recipe to pickle the sea bream with kelp and press it with the radish. The brilliant color of the radish seeing through the pressed sushi gives a figurative style to your dish.

Ingredients (for the mold at
20 x 7 x 4 cm/7.87 x 2.75 x 1.57 in. in size)

Sea Bream Pickled with the Kelp

Approx. 80 g/2.82 oz. sea bream
   for *sashimi*

20 cm/7.87 in. kelp

3 pieces radish

5 pieces green perilla

680 g/23.98 oz. sushi rice (see page 8)

1   Make the sea bream pickled with kelp first. Half-freeze the bream meat for about an hour in the freezer.

2   Wipe the both sides of the kelp with vinegar (not listed in the ingredients) with the wet washcloth and lay them on the vat. Cut #1 into thin slices, lay them on the kelp, and cover them with the cling film (see photo a). Put the vat in the refrigerator for 1–2 hours.

3   Cut the radish into thin slices, sprinkle the salt (not listed in the ingredients) a little, and leave it approximately for 10 minutes. Squeeze water out lightly.

4   Wet the mold, put the half amount of sushi rice, and level the surface. Press the surface with the pressing lid firmly. Tear the green perilla and place them on the sushi rice over all. Add the balance half of the sushi rice on the green perilla (see photo b) and level the surface.

5   Place the sliced radish on the surface over all, lay the sea bream meat by overlapping a little (see photo c) and cover the surface with the cling film. Press the surface with the pressing lid firmly (see photo d).

6   Remove the sushi body from the mold and cut them into pieces for an easy bite.

a

b

c

d

▪▪ Fish and Mixed Vegetables

This pressed sushi is a perfect menu for any festive occasions, with seafood such as boiled shrimps and broiled cod roe, as well as the mixed vegetables like *shiitake* mushrooms and the burdock with sweet soy sauce flavoring, green beans, fish pastes, and the julienned strips of thin omelets. Concealing the seaweed under the ingredients makes the whole taste of this sushi more distinct.

a   b

Ingredients (for the mold at
21.5 x 11.5 x 5 cm/8.46 x 4.52 x 1.96 in. in size)

8 pieces boiled shrimp

1 piece cod roe (small)

Shiitake Mushroom and Burdock with
Sweet Soy Sauce Flavoring

6 pieces dried *shiitake* mushroom

150 g/5.29 oz. burdock

150 ml reconstituted liquid from the
dried mushroom

1¹/₂ Tbs. each *sake*, soy sauce, sugar

2 pieces fish paste (pink)

2 pieces thin omelet to make
julienned strips (see page 10)

2–3 pieces boiled green bean
(see page 14)

850 g/29.98 oz. sushi rice

1 sheet toasted seaweed

1 Make the *shiitake* mushroom and
gourd with sweet soy sauce flavoring
first. Reconstitute the *shiitake*
mushroom with 300 ml of water.
Cut them into thin slices and keep
the reconstituted liquid. Shake off the

burdock's skin and cut it into long
thin shavings.

2 Pour the reconstituted liquid, *sake*,
soy sauce, and sugar and bring
them to a boil. Skim off the scum.
Cook over a light to medium flame
for 5–6 minutes until the liquid is
almost reduced to none. Drain the
ingredients in the colander.

3 Boil the shrimps with the hot
water including a sprinkling of
vinegar and salt (not listed in the
ingredients). Broil the cod roe and
flake the flesh away. Cut the fish
paste into strips. Cut the boiled
green beans into diagonally
thin slices.

4 Wet the mold, put the half amount
of sushi rice, and level the surface.
Press the surface with the pressing
lid firmly. Place #3 on the sushi
rice over all (see photo a). Add the
balance half of the sushi rice on the
green beans and level the surface.
Tear the seaweed with your hands

and spread it over the surface.

5 Scatter the julienned strips of thin
omelets and #3 over #4, taking into
the color balance of each ingredient.
Spread the cling film over the
surface and press the surface with
the pressing lid firmly (see photo
b). Put a weight on it and leave it for
20–30 minutes.

6 Remove the sushi body from the
mold and cut them into pieces for
an easy bite.

Plain Rice Sushi *Yurei Zushi*

Yurei means the ghost in Japanese. Plain rice sushi is supposed to be in the square shape with the plain (white) sushi rice only without mixing or topping any ingredients (featureless); thus its characteristic compares to the ghost. It indicates the fact that the plain rice is delicious enough without any additions.

Here on this page is the modern version of the ghost sushi. The front face is the pure white sushi rice while the ingredients are hidden underneath. In the Japanese ghost story, the ghost's companion is the willow tree. Cut the cucumber into thin strips, peel its skin, and decorate it on the plain white side of this sushi, resembling it as the willow leaves.

Ingredients (for the mold at
21.5 x 11.5 x 5 cm/8.46 x 4.52 x 1.96 in. in size)

30 g/1.05 oz. burdock

20 g/0.70 oz. carrot

1/2 piece deep-fried *tofu*

30 g/1.05 oz. edible wild plant boiled plain

100 ml soup stock

1 Tbs. soy sauce

1 Tbs. sugar

850 g/29.98 oz. sushi rice (see page 8)

2 pieces thin omelet to make julienned strips (see page 10)

30 g/1.05 oz. cod fish seasoned and flaked (*sakura denbu*)

1/2 piece cucumber skin

1 Shave off the burdock's skin and peel the one for the carrot. Boil the deep-fried *tofu* for 1–2 minutes or pour the hot water on to its surface, to remove the excess oil. Drain the water off from the edible wild plants boiled plain. Cut everything mentioned here off into cubes at 5 mm/0.19 in. in size.

2 Pour the stock, soy sauce, and sugar into the pan. Bring them to a boil, pour #1, and stir them while cooking over a light to medium flame for 4–5 minutes, until the liquid is almost reduced to none. Drain the ingredients in the colander.

3 Cut the cucumber skins into strips.

4 Split the sushi rice with the portions of 450 g/15.87 oz. and 400 g/14.19 oz. respectively. Add #2 to the bigger portion and mix.

5 Wet the mold, put the sushi rice with ingredients, and level the surface. Press the surface with the pressing lid firmly (photo a).

6 Spread the julienned strips of the omelets over #5 and place the cod fish seasoned and flaked. Add the plain rice over the ingredients (see photo b). Cover the surface with the cling film and press it with the pressing lid firmly.

7 Remove the sushi body from the mold and cut it into pieces for an easy bite. Place the cucumber skins as a decoration on the top surface.

a

b

◈ Roasted Beef

This easy yet festive recipe uses the roasted beef commercially available.
The key to the right taste is the special sauce made from the horseradish,
mayonnaise, and mustard.

Ingredients (for the mold at
  15 x 7 x 5 cm/5.90 x 2.75 x 1.96 in. in size)

250 g/8.81 oz. roasted beef
(commercially available, cutting into
thin slices)

Sauce

1 Tbs. grated horseradish

1 Tbs. mayonnaise

1 Ts. french mustard

1 Ts. vinegar

A sprinkling of salt and paper

510 g/17.98 oz. sushi rice (see page 8)

1 Mix the sauce ingredients.

2 Wet the mold, put the ²/₃ amount of
the sushi rice, and level the surface.
Press the surface with the pressing
lid firmly. Apply the half amount of
the sauce on the rice and spread the
half amount of roasted beef.

3 Add the rest of the sushi rice and
level the surface. Leaving a small
amount of the sauce for finishing,
apply it on the rice, and layer the
rest of the roasted beef again. Cover
the surface with the cling film and

press it with the pressing lid firmly.

4 Remove the sushi body from the
mold and use up the remaining of
the sauce. Cut it into pieces for an
easy bite.

❖ Smoked Salmon and Cheese in Pressed Trout Sushi Style

This recipe is the casual adaptation of the pressed sushi using the Camembert cheese package as a mold. Add the squeezed lemon juice in the sushi rice, so the finished sushi has a refreshing touch. The black pepper gives a good punch to its flavor.

Ingredients (for 1 package of the Camembert cheese at 13 cm/5.11 in. in size)

4–5 pieces smoked salmon

$^1/_3$ portion of full Camembert cheese

A sprinkling of black pepper

300 g/10.58 oz. sushi rice (see page 8)

Vinegar-based Sushi Dressing

1 Tbs. lemon squeezed juice

$^1/_2$ Tbs. vinegar

$^1/_2$ Tbs. sugar

$^1/_2$ Ts. salt

4–5 pieces bamboo leaf

1. Remove the thick part of the film yeast from the Camembert cheese and cut it into pieces at 5 mm/0.19 in. for the width.

2. Mix the ingredients of the vinegar-based sushi dressing and cool it down.

3. Wipe the surface of the bamboo leaves lightly and spread them radially on the bottom of the cheese package. Place the half amount of #2 and press it firmly with your hands. Place #1 on the surface, and sprinkle the black pepper (see photo).

4. Spread the rest of #2 and cover the surface with the smoked salmon.

5. Fold the bamboo leaves outside of the cheese package into the inside, cover the surface with the cling film, and close the box lid. Put a vat or the similar utensils as a weight on the package. Leave it for about 15 minutes to let it rest. Cut it into pieces for an easy bite.

Round Sushi Rice with Stripped Vegetables

Die cut the sushi rice with the round mold, wrap it around with the stripped vegetables, and add everybody's favorite salad on the top. Consider the color variations of the vegetables to combine, so the finished dishes highlight your meal table.

| Corned Beef Mayonnaise | Tuna Corn Mayonnaise | Crabmeat Mayonnaise |

Ingredients (for 2 round molds at
  6 cm/2.36 in. in size)

1 piece asparagus (thick)

6 pieces carrot in ribbon-shaped
  slices using the peeler

6 pieces zucchini (yellow) in
  ribbon-shaped slices using the peeler

Corned Beef Mayonnaise

$^1/_2$ small canned corned beef

1 Tbs. purple onion minced

1 Tbs. mayonnaise

A sprinkling of salt and pepper

Tuna Corn Mayonnaise

1 small canned tuna

2 Tbs. canned or pouched corn

1 Tbs. mayonnaise

A sprinkling of salt and pepper

Crabmeat Mayonnaise

$^1/_2$ small canned crabmeat

1 Tbs. mayonnaise

A sprinkling of salt and pepper

510 g/17.98 oz. sushi rice (see page 8)

A sprinkling of paprika powder and
  pink pepper

1 Cut the asparagus into ribbon-shaped slices using the peeler, dip it in hot water, and pour it into the colander to wipe off the excess water. Do the same for the carrots and zucchini.

2 Make the corned beef mayonnaise. Put the corned beef in the bowl and flake the meat away. Add the purple onion, mayonnaise, salt, and pepper to mix.

3 Make the tuna corn mayonnaise. Put the tuna in the bowl and flake the meat away. Add the corns, mayonnaise, salt, and pepper to mix.

4 Make the crabmeat mayonnaise. Put the crabmeat in the bowl and flake the meat away. Add the mayonnaise, salt, and pepper to mix.

5 Wet the mold, put the $^1/_6$ amount of the sushi rice, and die cut from the mold (see photo a). Make the same for 5 more sets.

6 Wrap the 2 strips each of the asparagus, carrot, and zucchini around the die-cut sushi rice (see photo b). Top #2 on the asparagus sushi and decorate it with the Italian parsley. Do #3 on the carrot sushi and sprinkle the paprika powder. Do #4 on the zucchini sushi and sprinkle the ground pink pepper.

a  b

Tuna Corn Mayonnaise

Corned Beef Mayonnaise

Crabmeat Mayonnaise

❖ Sushi in the Glass

With two kinds of sushi rice and ingredients, sushi in the glass is the spin-off sushi recipe in the hors d'oeuvre style. The key to the successful finish is to stuff rice and ingredients in the neat layers looking from the sideway as well.

Ingredients (for 4 glasses)

50 g/1.76 oz. lean tuna for *sashimi*

1 Ts. soy sauce

8 pieces peeled shrimp

2 Tbs. salmon roe

2 pieces egg to make the
scrambled egg (see page 11)

80 g/2.82 oz. mixed beans
(canned or pouched)

680 g/23.98 oz. sushi rice (see page 8)

2 Tbs. flaked salmon
(commercially available)

2–4 pieces boiled snow pea
(see page 14)

1–2 leaves green perilla

1 Cut lean tuna into small cubes, add soy sauce (see photo a), and mix them together. Boil the peeled shrimps in water with a pinch of vinegar and salt (not included in the ingredients).

2 Divide sushi rice into 2 equal portions. Mix the flaked salmon with the 1 portion of sushi rice.

3 Put the sushi rice with the flaked salmon into the glass, press the surface gently, and place the mixed beans (see photo b) on top. Put the other portion of sushi rice on and press the surface gently.

4 Put the fine-scrambled eggs on the sushi rice from #3 and add the lean tuna from #1, as well as the salmon roe. Chop the boiled snow peas or green perilla in half and decorate on top.

a

b

▪▪ Sushi in Flan Style

Sushi in flan style is pressed sushi made using pudding molds and eaten with spoons.
There are two flavors. One uses curry-flavored sushi rice with flaked meat, and
the other uses sushi rice mixed with scrambled eggs and broiled conger eel.
I tried to reproduce the look and shape of the flan through these combinations.

Flaked Meat with
Curry Powder

Conger Eel and
Scrambled Eggs

a

b

Ingredients (for 4 pieces of the pudding
mold at 5.5 cm/2.16 in. in diameter
and height in size)

Flaked Meat with Curry Powder

80 g/2.82 oz. beef ground with pork

$^1/_3$ Ts. salad oil

1 Ts. each sugar and *miso*

$^1/_3$ Ts. soy sauce

340 g/11.99 oz. sushi rice (see page 8)

1 Ts. curry powder

Conger Eel and Scrambled Eggs

100 g/3.52 oz. for a small piece,
conger eel

$1^1/_3$ Tbs. soy-based eel sauce
(commercially available)

340 g/11.99 oz. sushi rice (see page 8)

2 pieces egg to make the
scrambled egg (see page 11)

1 Make sushi in flan style with the
flaked meat with curry powder.
Pour the salad oil into the heated
frying pan and stir-fry the ground
meat. Season the meat with the
sugar, *miso*, and soy sauce and
stir-fry further until the seasonings
are dispersed.

2 Mix the curry powder with the
sushi rice.

3 Apply a dollop of the salad oil (not
listed in the ingredients) on the
inner side of the pudding mold,
put the $^1/_4$ amount of #1, and press
the $^1/_4$ amount of #2 (see photo a).
Press the surface firmly. Repeat this
process for 3 more pieces.

4 Place #3 on upside down, shake the
mold and ingredients (photo b), and
squeeze out the contents.

5 Make sushi in flan style with the
conger eel and scrambled eggs.
Roughly chop the conger eel.

6 Add the scrambled egg in the sushi
rice and mix.

7 Apply a dollop of the salad oil (not
listed in the ingredients) on the
inner side of the pudding mold, put
the $^1/_4$ amount of #5, and press the
$^1/_4$ of #6. Press the surface firmly.
Repeat this process for 3 more
pieces. Squeeze out the contents just
like you did for #4, and pour the eel
sauce.

◆ Cubed Sushi

Cubed sushi is the recipe in the finger-food style, using the cubed ice trays as the molds.
Sushi rice with the mix of various cereals can be prepared just in the same way you usually
mix the freshly cooked rice with the rice vinegar-based sushi dressing (*awasezu*).
Apply cream cheese as the topping so that you can serve as the appetizer.

Ingredients (at the amount of your choice)

10 g/0.35 oz young sardine (*jako*)

A pinch of sesame oil

$^1/_2$ Ts. roasted sesame seed

Dried food sprinkled over rice
a few variations

Parsley Cream Cheese

30 g/1.05 oz. cream cheese

1 Ts. each chopped parsley, milk

Red Perilla Cream Cheese

30 g/1.05 oz. cream cheese

$^1/_3$ Ts. dried and powdered
red perilla (*yukari*)

1 Ts. milk

340 g/11.99 oz sushi rice with the mix of
various cereals (see page 8)

1 Frizzle the young sardines and
   mix it with the sesame.

2 Mix each ingredient for the
   parsley cream cheese and red perilla
   cream cheese.

3 Wet the cubed ice trays with water
   and press the two kinds of sushi rice
   respectively. Use the back face of
   the spoon for pressing tightly.
   Remove the sushi rice from the
   cubed ice trays.

4 For the standard sushi rice, sprinkle
   #1 and dried and powdered food.
   For the one with various cereals, mix
   either one of the ingredients in #2.
   Push toothpicks into the finished
   sushi when necessary.

▩ Crabmeat and Avocado Burger Sushi

This recipe is the over-sized burger sushi, likened the sushi rice to buns. Fillings are avocado, thick slices of tomatoes, crabmeat while using flying fish roes as the topping. Pour the aurora sauce over it, and it is ready.

Ingredients (for 2 pieces)

$^1/_2$ piece avocado

$^1/_2$ piece large fruit tomato

200 g/7.05 oz. peeled crabmeat

1 Tbs. flying fish roe

A pinch of cayenne pepper

510 g/17.98 oz. sushi rice (see page 8)

Aurora Sauce

3 Tbs. mayonnaise

1 Tbs. tomato ketchup

1 Ts. water

A pinch of salt and pepper

1 Remove the skin and seeds of avocado and slice the meat into the thickness of 1 cm/0.39 in. Slice the tomato into the same size. Flake the crabmeat.

2 Place the cling film onto the vat, put the round mold at 9 cm/3.54 in. in diameter, and press approximately $^1/_4$ amount of sushi rice. Press the sushi rice hard using the back face of spoons, and remove it from the molds. Prepare for the 2 sets of this step.

3 Put the round mold again, but in one smaller size than #2 (approximately 8 cm/3.14 in.) onto the same vat, press the sushi rice hard, and remove it from the mold.

Prepare for the 2 sets of this step.

4 Place the sushi rice in #2 respectively onto the dish, layer the tomato and avocado in order, sprinkle the half amount of crabmeat and place the sushi rice in #3. Top the rest of the crabmeat, mix the ingredients of the aurora sauce, and pour it onto the sushi rice. Sprinkle the flying fish roes and the cayenne pepper.

⬚ Round Cake Sushi

Round cake sushi is the pressed sushi in the round shape, using the ring mold at 15 cm/5.90 in. in diameter in size. Decorate the top with salmon, salmon roe, julienned strips of thin omelets, a couple of green vegetables, and cherry tomatoes. It could be a good example that you can make a festive sushi dish with the familiar ingredients only.

Ingredients (for 1 piece of the ring mold for baking cakes, at 15 cm/5.90 in. in diameter)

50 g/1.76 oz. salmon for *sashimi*, cutting into thin slices

2 Tbs. salmon roe

2 pieces thin omelet, cutting into thick strips (see page 10)

5–8 pieces snow pea (see page 14)

4–6 pieces broccoli in small size

4–8 pieces cherry tomato

Appropriate amount of mayonnaise

680 g/23.98 oz. sushi rice (see page 8)

5 g/0.17 oz. toasted seaweed cut into strips

1 Boil the broccoli in hot water with a sprinkle of salt (not listed in the ingredients). Cut snow peas diagonally into slices. Remove the calyx of the cherry tomato.

2 Apply a dollop of the salad oil (not listed in the ingredients) on the inner side of the ring mold. Put the half amount of sushi rice and level the surface. Cover surface with the cling film and press firmly (see photo a). Remove the cling film and scatter the seaweed over all.

3 Put the rest of the sushi rice on #2 and level the surface. Cover the surface with the cling film, press it firmly, and remove the cling film.

4 Place #3 upside down on the dish.

Push the bottom of the mold while lifting it up slowly, and press the contents off (see photo b & c). Remove the lower part of the frame too (see photo d).

5 Spread the julienned strips of the thin omelets, leaving the space at the edge of sushi rice.

6 Roll up the 2 each piece of the salmon flesh in the shape of flower petals, top them on the surface. Place the salmon roe in the center of the salmon petals and add pieces of the snow peas.

7 Squeeze the mayonnaise out around a few places where the julienned strips of thin omelets are. Place the broccoli and cherry tomatoes.

a

b

c

d

Pressed Sushi

❖ Terrine Sushi

Pressed sushi using the terrine mold has a hint of the European taste and is in fact a good match to the wines. Wrapping the ingredients with the raw ham maintains a clean shape. Keep in mind how the cross section looks like when cutting into pieces and make sure there are no extra spaces in-between each ingredient.

Ingredients (for 1 piece of the terrine mold at 17 x 8 x 6.5 cm/6.69 x 3.14 x 2.55 in.)

70 g/2.46 oz. soft and thin slices of raw ham

4–6 pieces boiled shrimp (see page 14)

$^1/_4$–$^1/_2$ piece red and yellow paprika

24 pieces asparagus

6–7 pieces gumbo

4–6 pieces canned or pouched baby corn

680 g/23.98 oz. sushi rice (see page 8)

1 Place the paprika on the grill without peeling off the skin and broil them over the high heat for 3–4 minutes, until the top skins are scorched black. Turn down the paprika and keep broiling for another 1–2 minutes. Let it cool down, peel off the skin, and slice it vertically into half.

2 Cut off the hard roots of the asparagus. Remove the calyx of the gumbo. Dip both of them in hot water with a sprinkle of salt (not listed in the ingredients) for 1 minute, pour them into the cold water, and wipe off the excess water.

3 Spread the cling film larger than the mold in size tightly on the terrine mold, leaving the excess part of the film outside. Spread the raw ham by making layers, leaving the excess part of the meat to hang out from the mold.

4 Put the $^1/_4$ amount of sushi rice on #3 and press it tightly. Place the asparagus and baby corns on the surface, and another $^1/_4$ amount of sushi rice again. Level the surface.

5 Place the paprika evenly (see photo a), add the next $^1/_4$ amount of sushi rice and level the surface. Spread the boiled shrimps and gumbos and seal them with the last $^1/_4$ amount of sushi rice. Level the surface.

6 Fold the excess raw ham hanging inside and cover it with the cling film. Press the surface with your hands to level (see photo b). Put either thin board or another terrine mold, whose size is matching to the inside size of the first one, on the surface and let it rest.

7 Take out the body of the sushi from the terrine mold by lifting up the cling film. Cut into pieces for an easy bite.

a

b

Pressed Sushi

⚏ Wrapped and Pouched Sushi

The lovely look of the tiny sushi balls has always been the highlight
of the festive table since the old days in Japan.
Like the bright egg color of the sushi balls in egg layer,
colorful vegetable sushi *Tosa* style, or *tofu* pushes,
the wrapped and pouched sushi plays a key role in the going
on the excursion. Easy to bite, a feast for the eyes,
they are pretty on the plates or stored in the lunch boxes.

Tiny Sushi Balls *Temari Zuzhi*

Temari is the hand-made balls for children to play. The lovely sushi balls borrow the colors and shapes of small cotton balls which have been a play equipment for centuries in Japan. The examples on this spread use the sea bream, salmon, and calamari, but you can alternate with other seafood, such as lean tuna, smoked salmon, or shrimps. Bear in your mind to select as colorful variations of the ingredients as possible. Tiny sushi balls are perfect for guest-welcoming opportunities or *hanami* parties too.

Ingredients (for 4 pieces each)

8 pieces salmon for *sashimi* cut into thin slices

8 pieces kisslip cuttlefish for *sashimi* cut into thin slices

8 pieces sea bream for *sashimi* cut into thin slices

A sprinkling of salt

680 g/23.98 oz. sushi rice (see page 8)

A sprinkling of dill, sliced lemon, sliced red paprika, parched black sesame

4 pieces leaf bud of Japanese pepper

1. Split the sushi rice proportionally equal to 12 portions and make rice balls.

2. Spread the cling film, place the 2 pieces of the salmon flesh with their ventral sides facing down, and top #1 (see photo a). Wrap it with the cling film and twist the top (see photo b) to organize the shape (see photo c). Repeat this process for 3 more pieces of the sushi ball.

3. Repeat the #2 process for the kisslip cuttlefish and sea bream.

4. Top the dill and small pieces of the sliced lemon for salmon, red paprika for the kisslip cuttlefish, and the leaf bud of the Japanese pepper for the sea bream. Add soy sauce, to taste.

a

b

c

Sushi Balls in Egg Layer, Tea-cloth Style *Chakin Zushi*
Sushi Balls in Egg Layer, Crape-wrapper Style *Fukusa Zushi*

Both types use the thick omelet and sushi rice with the mixed ingredients.
When wrapped in omelets made like the tea-cloth, it is the sushi balls in egg layer, tea-cloth style. Same is applied for the crape-wrapper style.
I have tied up the finished sushi balls with the boiled Japanese honewort for the recipe in this spread, but you can also use the boiled gourd instead.

Ingredients (for 2 pieces each)

250 g/8.81 oz. sushi rice (see page 8)

2 pieces boiled shrimp

4 pieces boiled Japanese honewort

30 g/1.05 oz. boiled gourd (see page 13)

$^1/_2$ sheet toasted seaweed

4 pieces thin omelet (see page 10. Finished size is 22 cm/8.66 in.)

2 grains green pea, canned or pouched

1 Boil the shrimps with hot water with a sprinkling of vinegar and salt (not listed in the ingredients).

2 Cook the Japanese honewort lightly without cutting its length, and squeeze out the excess water.

3 Chop the boiled gourd finely. Tear the seaweed sheet into pieces. Pour the sushi rice in the bowl, add #2, and mix (see photo a). Split it into 4 equal portions.

4 Make the sushi balls in egg layer, tea-cloth style. Spread the thin omelet on the bowl in a relatively small size, make the round ball from #3 (see photo b), and tuck the omelet in the center. Tie the sushi body with the Japanese honewort (see photo c). Top the boiled shrimp and green peas.

5 Make the sushi balls in egg layer, crape-wrapper style. Spread the thin egg omelet in the smaller container and shape the sushi rice in #3 in a rectangle. Place the sushi rice on the foreground side, fold the left and right sides of the thin omelet to tuck them in for wrapping (see photo d). Tie the finished sushi balls with the Japanese honewort.

a

b

c

d

Sushi Balls in Egg Layer, Tea-cloth Style

Sushi Balls in Egg Layer, Crape-wrapper Style

71

▪ *Sushi Burrito*

Ingredients (for 2 pieces each)

Bite-sized Cutlet and Cabbage Salad

1 sheet for pork medallion to make bite-sized cutlet

2 Tbs. each flour and water

Appropriate amount of bread crumbs and frying oil

200 g/7.05 oz. cabbage cut into strips

¼ piece paprika (red) cut into strips

Appropriate amount of salt and pepper

1 Tbs. vinegar

40 g/1.41 oz. corn canned or pouched

1 Ts. mayonnaise

1 Tbs. brown sauce for breaded pork cutlets

340 g/11.99 oz. sushi rice (see page 8)

2 sheets toasted seaweed

Roasted Pork, Carrot and Avocado Salad

150 g/5.29 oz. minced pork meat

½ Ts. salad oil

1½ Tbs. sauce for barbecued meat

1 piece carrot cut into strips

⅓ Ts. salt

1 Tbs. vinegar

½ Tbs. olive oil

A sprinkling of pepper

1 Tbs. mayonnaise

½ piece avocado cut into slices

340 g/11.99 oz. sushi rice (see page 8)

2 sheets toasted seaweed

Bite-sized Cutlet and Cabbage Salad

Roasted Pork and Avocado with Salad

1. Make bite-sized cutlet and cabbage salad first. Halve the pork meat and tenderize it with the kitchen mallet. Pour the flours in the bowl and add 2 Tbs. of water and salt, and a sprinkling of pepper to mix. Dip the pork meat in the same bowl to disperse, coat it with the bread crumbs next, and deep-fry it in the oil for 2–3 minutes per side until golden brown.

2. Sprinkle the ⅓ Ts. of salt and vinegar over the cabbage and paprika, leave them for 15 minutes to squeeze out the excess water. Add corns and marinate all of them with mayonnaise, and a sprinkling of pepper to taste.

3. Place the seaweed over the bamboo rolling mat and spread the sushi rice leaving the space at 1–2 cm/0.39–0.78 in. at the far side. Place #2 after squeezing out the excess water on the foreground, and pork meat after applying the brown sauce for breaded port cutlet on the one side only (see photo a). Fold the ingredients altogether into half (see photo b).

4. Wrap #3 with the oven sheet (see photos c & d) and twist the edges (see photo e). Halve them to make 2 pieces.

5. Make the roasted pork, carrots and avocado salad. Stir-fry the pork in the oil heated in the frying pan and season it with the sauce for barbecued pork cutlet.

6. Marinate the carrots well with salt, vinegar, olive oil, pepper, and mayonnaise.

7. Place the seaweed over the bamboo rolling mat and spread the sushi rice leaving the space at 1–2 cm/0.39–0.78 in. at the far side. Place #6 after squeezing out the excess water on the foreground, #5, and avocado. Fold the ingredients altogether into the half.

8. Wrap #7 with the oven sheet and twist the edges. Halve them to make 2 pieces.

a

b

c

d

e

Wrapped and Pouched Sushi

Burrito is a type of the Mexican food, wrapping up the meats, vegetables, and avocado with the tortillas, a thin layer of the skin made from the flour. Here in this spread, instead of the tortillas, I used the sushi rice and seaweed wrapped further with the oven sheet. This is what we can call, the Japanese burrito.

Roasted Pork, Carrot and
Avocado Salad

Bite-sized Cutlet and
Cabbage Salad

Beef Wrapped Sushi

I came up with this recipe as the arrangement of the beef-wrapped rice balls.
Wrap the sushi rice with beef meat, broil it with the salad pan, and marinate it with
sweetened soy sauce. Either cramming the hot and ready one in your mouth
or cutting into pieces for an easy bite after cooling it down is your choice.

Ingredients (for 4 pieces)

200 g/7.05 oz. beef round cut into slices

340 g/11.99 oz. sushi rice (see page 8)

20 g/0.70 oz. red pickled ginger

1 Tbs. white parched sesame

1 Ts. salad oil

Sweetened Soy Sauce

1 Tbs. *sake*

1 Tbs. soy sauce

1 Tbs. sugar

1. Chop the red pickled ginger into pieces and mix it together with the sesame in the sushi rice.
2. Split #1 into 4 equal portions and make each into the rice balls in the cylinder shape.
3. Spread 1–2 sheets of the beef round on the cutting board by layering, place #2 in the foreground, roll it down to the far side (see photo a), and wrap the whole rice balls with the beef round.
4. Heat the frying pan with the salad oil, and line #3 side by side, with its closing point facing down. Roll over #3 time to time for 4–5 minutes per side until golden brown.
5. Mix the ingredients for the sweetened soy sauce together and pour the sauce evenly into #4. Let the sauce reduce until it is well marinated.
6. Cram the finished piece in your mouth or cut them into pieces for an easy bite.

a

b

Vegetable Sushi, Tosa Country Style

Ingredients (for 4 pieces each)

Cooked Arum Root

120 g/4.23 oz. arum root

150 ml soup stock

1 Tbs. each soy sauce, sugar

Cooked Bamboo Shoot

80 g/2.82 oz. bamboo shoot
(Henon bamboo is most desirable,
but the alternative should be okay)

100 ml soup stock

1 Tbs. each light soy sauce,
sweetened *sake*

Sweet and Sour Lotus Root Pickles

80 g/2.82 oz. lotus root
(for stem parts)

1 Tbs. each soup stock, vinegar

$^1/_2$ Tbs. sugar

A sprinkling of salt

Grilled *Shiitake* Mushroom

4 pieces *shiitake* mushroom

A sprinkling of soy source

4 pieces *myoga* pickled in the
sweetened vinegar (see page 15)

680 g/23.98 oz. freshly cooked rice

50 ml citron vinegar

$1^1/_2$ Tbs. sugar

$^2/_3$ Ts. salt

1 Make the cooked arum root first.
Cut the arum into slices at 7–8
mm/0.27–0.31 in., make slits inside
to open it flat (see photo a), and
boil it in hot water. Drain the excess
water in the colander. Pour the soup
stock, soy sauce and sugar in the pot
and bring them to a boil, add the
arum to simmer for 4–5 minutes.
Leave it to cool down.

2 Make the cooked bamboo shoot.
Remove the hard core inside of the
bamboo. Pour the soup stock and
sweetened *sake* in the pot and bring
them to a boil, add the bamboo
shoot to simmer for 4–5 minutes.
Leave it to cool down.

3 Make the sweet and sour lotus
root pickles. Cut the lotus root
into pieces at 4 cm/1.57 in. in size
and peel off the skin (see photo b).
Cut it vertically into 5 mm/0.19
in. in thickness and coat it with a
sprinkling of salt. Boil it in the hot
water quickly, pour it in the cold
water, and squeeze it out for the
excess water. Mix the soup stock,
vinegar, sugar, and salt to make
the pickled liquid. Pour the lotus
in the liquid.

4 Make grilled *shiitake* mushroom.
Cut off the stem, broil it per side
until golden brown. Dip it in the
soy sauce.

5 Mix the citron vinegar, sugar, and
salt and pour the liquid evenly over
the rice cooked freshly (see photo c).
Stuff it in the #2 equally (see photo
d) at the appropriate amount. For
the rest of the sushi rice, split into 16
portions evenly and make sushi balls
in the shape of the rice bag.

6 Wrap the sushi balls with the
ingredients for #3 and #4, just like
you do for hand-shaped sushi (see
photo e). Halve the *myoga* vertically
and use the outer and bigger skin
only to wrap. Press the sushi rice
into the slits for #1 (see photo f).

Wrapped and Pouched Sushi

Tosa is the old name of the *Kochi* prefecture
where it has been famous for the vegetable sushi for a long time.
Combine the riches of the soil together, such as the bamboo shoots,
giant elephant ears, *myoga*, *shiitake* mushrooms,
they are rich in taste and pleasing to the eyes.
Sushi rice with the citron matches well to the vegetable sushi.

❖ Cherry Leaves Wrapped Sushi

Mix the pickled plum and red radish with the sushi rice, shape it like the cherry leaf rice cake (*sakura mochi*), and cover the sushi with the salted cherry leaves.

Enjoy the charming look reminiscent of the original rice cake. It goes well with *sake* too.

Ingredients (for 4–6 pieces)

1 piece pickled plum

20 g/0.70 oz. pickled red radish

340 g/11.99 oz. freshly cooked rice

1 Ts. white parched sesame

4–6 pieces salted cherry leaf

1 Remove the seed from the pickled plum and crush it. Mince the pickled red radish.

2 Pour the rice into the bowl, add #1 and mix. Split it into the 4–6 portions equally, make the round and flat balls, and sprinkle the white parched sesame.

3 Wrap #2 with the salted cherry blossom leaves.

❏ *Leaf Mustard Wrapped Sushi* Mehari Zushi

The origin of the leaf mustard wrapped sushi is the rice balls for the excursion lunch box in the *Kumano* and *Nanki* area, *Wakayama* prefecture. The size of this sushi is therefore huge due to the original purpose. The sesame or dried young sardines gives an additional taste to this simple sushi dish.

Ingredients (for 4 pieces)

80 g/2.82 oz. pickled leaf mustard
 (choose the fresh green leaves.)

2 g/0.07 oz. bonito flakes

A sprinkling of soy sauce

340 g/11.99 oz. sushi rice (see page 8)

1 Check the taste of the pickled leaf mustard first. If it is too salty, dip it in the water for approx. 10 minutes to drain the excess salt. Separate it into the stems and leaves.

2 Mince the stems and mix them with the bonito flake. Add salt to mix again.

3 Split the sushi rice into the 4 portions equally. Stuff #2 in the center and make the rice balls.

4 Spread the leaves of the leaf mustard, put #3 on the center, and wrap it up.

❖ Persimmon Leaves Wrapped Sushi *Kakinoha Zushi*

The origin of the persimmon leaves wrapped sushi is the local sushi in *Nara* and *Wakayama* prefectures. Here in my applied recipe, wrap the salmon, pickled horse mackerel, and sushi rice with the persimmon leaves. Our ancestors taught us that the persimmon leaves have bactericidal action. Covering the sushi rice with the leaves is logical enough, not just to prevent it from the dryness.

Ingredients (for 12 pieces)

Pickled Horse Mackerel (at the amount of your choice)

2 pieces horse mackerel for *sashimi* (prepare to make a slit along the length, cut the symmetrical right and left halves, leaving the backbone.)

1 Tbs. salt

Approx. 100 ml vinegar

Pickled Salmon

80 g/2.82 oz. frozen fillet of salmon

1 Tbs. salt

Approx. 100 ml vinegar

360 g/12.69 oz. sushi rice

12 pieces persimmon leaf (remove the stems in advance)

Appropriate amount of *myoga* in sweetened vinegar (see page 15)

1 Make the pickled horse mackerel. Spread the half amount of salt on the vat, place the prepared mackerels, and sprinkle the rest of salt evenly (see photo a). Leave it for approx. 15 minutes. Wash away the salt lightly, wipe off the excess water and place the mackerels to another vat. Add the vinegar and dip the mackerels, leaving for approx. 15 minutes (see photo b).

2 Make pickled salmon in the same way as #1.

3 Shave off the ventral bones (see photo c), remove the small bones using the tweezers (see photo d), and peel off the skin (see photo e). Cut into thin slices, and do the same with the salmon.

4 Split the sushi rice into the portions of 30 g/1.05 oz. and hand-shape them into the lean shapes.

5 Direct the sharp edge of the persimmon leaves to the foreground, place #3 with the skin side facing down, and top #4 (see photo f). Roll it down from the foreground (see photo g) while folding the sides of the leaves, and stuck the finished sushi in the box or vat. Roll down the rest of #3 in the same way.

6 Place the weight or vat on the top of the sushi and keep it in the vegetable storage space in the refrigerators (the one being not too cool) for a few hours to rest. Add the *myoga* in sweetened vinegar.

 a

 b

 c

 d

 e

 f

 g

⚏ Tofu Pouches *Inari Zushi*

Tofu pouches are the standard version of the home-made sushi cookings.
Here in this spread, I am showing the 2 patterns of the pouch skins, one with the front
and the other on the back side of the deep-fried *tofu*. The key to the success of
this recipe is on the way to simmer the skins in the soup stock. Sushi rice variations for
recommendation include the fruits of the Japanese pepper or grated citron skins.

Ingredients (for 12 pieces)

6 pieces deep-fried *tofu*

266 ml soup stock

4 Tbs. soy sauce

3 1/2 Tbs. sugar

3 Tbs. sweetened *sake*

680 g/23.98 oz. sushi rice (see page 8)

1 Tbs. white parched sesame

1. Flatten the deep-fried *tofu* using the chopstick (see photo a), halve and open it in the form of pouch.

2. Boil the water in the pan, put #1 while holding firmly to squeeze out the excess fat, and put it in the colander to drain the excess water completely (see photo b).

3. Pour the soup stock, soy source, sugar, and sweetened *sake* in the pan, and bring them to a boil. Place #2 in circular layers, cover the surface with the drop-lid (see photos c & d), and simmer the ingredients for 12–13 minutes. While cooking, pay attention to the condition. You may want to pour the simmered liquid evenly. When the drop-lid is made of wood, press a little harder onto the surface, so that the *tofu* pouches absorb the soup well.

4. Keep simmering, and let it reduce the liquid until the *tofu* pouches absorb the seasonings. Turn off the heat (see photo e) and cool down the ingredients.

5. Add the white parched sesame with the sushi rice and mix them lightly (see photo f). Split the sushi rice into 12 portions equally and make sushi balls in the cylinder shape.

6. Once #4 gets cool down, squeeze it gently using your palms, and drain the excess liquid (see photo g). Turn the front side over for the half of the finished pouches.

7. Stuff #5 in #6 (see photo h) without spaces and fold the edges of the pouches inside.

a

b

c

d

e

f

g

h

Wrapped and Pouched Sushi

⠿ Baked Tofu Pouches

You don't have to boil down the *tofu* pouches like the recipe on the previous page,
but broil it on the direct flame and marinate with the noodle soup.
Stuff the sushi rice inside and top your favorite ingredients on.
This recipe is in more homely style with the savory smell of the *tofu* pouches.

Ingredients (for 4 pieces each)

6 pieces deep-fried *tofu*

Noodle Soup

4 Tbs. noodle stick (3-time concentrated)

2 Tbs. water

Asparagus and *Shimeji* Mushroom, Marinated with Cod Roe

2 pieces asparagus

50 g/1.76 oz. *shimeji* mushroom

20 g/0.70 oz. cod roe

Cooked Sausage and Zucchini

2 pieces sausage

¹/₃ slice zucchini

¹/₂ Ts. salad oil

A sprinkling of salt and pepper

Appropriate amount of mayonnaise

***Natto* and Grated Yam**

40 g/1.41 oz. *natto*

50 g/1.76 oz. yam

A sprinkling of green laver

510 g/17.98 oz. sushi rice (see page 8)

1　Flatten the deep-fried sushi using the chopstick, halve and open it in the form of pouch.

2　Pour the ingredients of the noodle soup either on vat or any other flat containers, and mix them well.

3　Turn on the broiler, lay #1, and broil the both sides to golden brown. Dip #1 in #2 while they are still hot (see photo a).

4　Make the asparagus and *shimeji* mushroom, marinated with cod roe. Cut the asparagus into pieces at 1 cm/0.39 in. and halve *shimeji* mushroom. Boil them together in hot water for approx. 1 minute and drain the water. Marinate them with the cod roe.

5　Make the cooked sausage and zucchini. Finely chop the sausages at 7–8 mm/0.27–0.31 in. in width, and organize the length of the zucchini

as the sausage. Pour the salad oil in the heated frying pan and stir-fry them together quickly. Sprinkle the salt and pepper.

6　Make *natto* and grated yam. Mix the seasonings (usually attached to the *natto* packs) with the kneaded mustard and *natto*. Peel off the skin of the yam and grate it.

7　Fold the edge of the *tofu* pouches inside a little (see photo b) and stuff the sushi rice in the equal amount. Place #4 for the first 4 pouches, and #5 on the next 4 and mayonnaise. Put the *natto* and yam ingredients on the last 4 pouches and sprinkle the green laver.

Asparagus and Shimeji
Mushroom, Marinated
with Cod Roe

Natto and
Grated Yam

Cooked Sausage
and Zucchini

⬛ Sushi in the Bowl

Sushi in the bowl is the sushi rice mixed or topped with the ingredients (*chirashi zushi*). There are many variations in this category, but the key to making the successful sushi dish is to consider using the seasonal ingredients promptly. The color combination of the rice and ingredients is also important. Using the western ingredients is also a good idea, as it gives a richer variety in your recipe.

Sushi in the Bowl *Bara Chirashi*

With a few variations of the *sashimi* cutting into the small dices and decorating them on the sushi rice, sushi in the bowl is the rich and perfect menu to entertain your guests or for the festive occasions. To dress up with the thick omelets, cucumbers, and leaf buds of the Japanese peppers creates a fancy and colorful piece of sushi art. Keep in mind to make all the ingredients to be visible when serving it on the table.

Ingredients (for 4 persons)

80 g/2.82 oz. lean tuna for *sashimi*

80 g/2.82 oz. salmon for *sashimi*

Japanese Horseradish Soy Sauce

1 Ts. grated Japanese horseradish

1 Tbs. soy sauce

1/2 piece roasted conger eel

3 pieces pickled gizzard shad (commercially available)

1/2 piece cucumber

Appropriate amount of thick omelet (see page 11)

2 Tbs. adductor

2 Tbs. cod roe

Appropriate amount of leaf buds of Japanese pepper

680 g/23.98 oz. of sushi rice (see page 8)

1　Dice the tuna and salmon at 1 cm/0.39 in. and put them into the bowl. Mix the ingredients of the Japanese horseradish soy sauce and marinate with the tuna and salmon (see photo a).

2　Put the roasted conger eel into the heat-resistant dish, sprinkle the 1 Ts. of *sake* (not listed in the ingredients), and cook it in the microwave for 1 minute. Dice it at 1 cm/0.39 in.

3　Dice the gizzard shad and cucumber at 7–8 mm/0.27–0.31 in, and the thick omelet in 1 cm/0.39 in.

4　Serve the sushi rice in the dish, scatter #1 and #2 on the rice (see photo b), and place the leaf buds of the Japanese pepper at random. Serve the Japanese horseradish soy sauce in the small plate.

a

b

Bonito Sushi in the Bowl

Bonito sushi in the bowl is the dynamic soul food in the *Ise Shima* area in *Mie* prefecture. The recipe is to dip the bonito in the sweetened soy sauce in advance and to mix it with sushi rice. The hint of the deliciousness is in the scent of the various garnishes, such as the ginger, green perilla, and young leaves of the versatile leeks. You can try to make this sushi with the lean tuna instead of the bonito.

Ingredients (for 4 persons)

300 g/10.58 oz. frozen fillets bonito for *sashimi*

Sweetened soy sauce

1 Tbs. soy sauce

1 Tbs. sweetened *sake*

20 g/0.70 oz. pickled ginger (see page 17)

3 Tbs. pickled liquid

4 pieces green perilla

20 g/0.70 oz. young leaf of versatile leek

680 g/23.98 oz. of freshly cooked rice

$^1/_2$ Tbs. each white and black parched sesame

1. Cut the bonito into slices at 7–8 mm/0.27–0.31 in. Pour the ingredients of the sweetened soy sauce and mix. Add the bonito in the sauce and leave it for approx. 10 minutes to disperse the seasonings (see photo a).

2. Cut the pickled gingers into strips, and green perilla in 7–8 mm/0.27–0.31 in. in a square. Chop off the roots of the young leaves of the versatile leeks.

3. Put the rice into the bowl and distribute the pickled liquid evenly (see photo b). You should use the rice paddle as if it slices through the rice. Cool it down.

4. Add #1 after draining the liquid to #3, and #2 and sesame leaving a small amount for the later decoration. Turn down the rice without kneading (photo c).

5. Serve the sushi in the dish and sprinkle the rest of the garnishes for decoration.

a

b

c

Vegetarian Sushi in the Bowl

Vegetarian sushi in the bowl is one of the most classic home-made sushi menus since the old days. It does not use the meats and seafood and consists of the vegetables, mushrooms, and soy products only. Simmer the vegetables, mushrooms, and freeze-dried *tofu* in the mild seasonings, and pickle the lotus root highlighting its white color. The green vegetables to scatter at the end of the cooking course also plays a key role. Serve it in the large dish so everyone can reach for one's share.

Ingredients (for 4–5 persons)

4 pieces *shiitake* mushroom

100 g/3.52 oz. *maitake* mushroom

50 g/1.76 oz. carrot

3 Tbs. *sake*

2 Tbs. soup stock

1 Tbs. soy sauce

1 Tbs. sugar

2 pieces freeze-dried *tofu* (see page 13)

80 g/2.82 oz. lotus root cut into decorative pieces (see page 15)

5 pieces boiled green bean (see page 14)

680 g/23.98 oz. sushi rice (see page 8)

1 Remove the stem of the *shiitake* mushrooms and cut into thin slices. Tear the *maitake* mushrooms by hands into pieces for an easy bite. Cut the carrots into fine and rectangular slices. Pour these ingredients into the pan, add the *sake*, soup stocks, soy sauce, and sugar. Put the seasonings over the fire with the low to medium flame. Stir the ingredients with the chopsticks to simmer (see photo a). Once the carrots are cooked well, turn off the heat.

2 Squeeze the liquid lightly out from the freeze-dried *tofu*, halve its thickness and cut it vertically. Cut the *tofu* further into strips at 5 mm/0.19 in. in width (see photo b).

3 Cut the green beans into diagonal slices.

4 Add #1 and #2 to the sushi rice and mix well.

5 Serve the sushi in the dish, and scatter #3 and lotus root cut into decorative pieces at random.

a

b

Beef and Burdock Sushi in the Bowl

Cooking the beef and the burdock together is the golden combination in the Japanese home cooking. This easy sushi is to stir-fry and then boil them in the sauce. The burdock absorbs the rich seasonings of the beef and is very delicious. Scatter the *benitade* at random and it is ready to enjoy.

Ingredients (for 4–5 persons)

200 g/7.05 oz. pieces of sliced beef

100 g/3.52 oz. burdock

1 Ts. salad oil

2 Tbs. *sake*

1 Tbs. soy sauce

1 Tbs. sugar

680 g/23.98 oz. sushi rice (see page 8)

15 g/0.52 oz. *benitade*

1 Cut the beef into slices for an easy bite.

2 Shave off the burdock's skin and cut it into long thin shaving. Dip it in the water and drain the excess water in the colander.

3 Heat the salad oil in the frying pan, add #2, and stir-fry over a medium flame. Once the burdock is translucent, add #1 and stir-fry further for approx. 2 minutes. Once the beef is nearly cooked, add the *sake*, soy source and sugar, and cook for another 2–3 minutes until the liquid is nearly reduced.

4 Add #3 to the sushi rice and mix without kneading.

5 Serve the ingredients into the dish and scatter a plenty amount of *benitade* at random.

Sushi in the Bowl

◼ Dried Barracuda Sushi in the Bowl

Broil the dried barracuda to golden brown, flake its flesh, and mix it in the sushi rice along with the *narazuke*, or pickled vegetables in *sake* lees. The additional *myoga* savory stimulates our appetites. You can replace the *narazuke* pickles to something else, such as parched sesame, the pickled fruits of the Japanese pepper, and green perilla or other similar garnishes.

Ingredients (for 4 persons)

1 piece barracuda salted and dried
  overnight at large size

40 g/1.41 oz. *narazuke* pickle

2–3 pieces *myoga*

500 g/17.63 oz. sushi rice (see page 8)

1 Broil the dried barracuda to golden brown, flake its flesh after removing the head and bones.

2 Remove the residue lee lightly from *narazuke* pickles. Mince it and chop the *myoga* finely.

3 Add #1 and #2 in the sushi rice, while leaving a little amount for the later decoration. Mix them without kneading.

4 Serve them in the dish, and scatter the rest of the garnishes at random.

⠿ Pickled Sea Bream and Chrysanthemum Petals Sushi in the Bowl

Pickled sea bream is the specialty of the *Wakasa Obama* district in *Fukui* prefecture.
It may not be easy to relish its authenticity without visiting there.
But if you are lucky enough to have a chance to get it in your nearby shopping malls,
buy one and try this menu.

Ingredients (for 2 persons)

40 g/1.41 oz. pickled sea bream
(commercially available)

Pickled Chrysanthemum Petals

20 g/0.70 oz. chrysanthemum petal

1 Tbs. vinegar

1 Ts. sugar

A sprinkling of salt

2 Tbs. salmon roe

340 g/11.99 oz. plain rice, freshly
cooked

1 Tbs. plum vinegar

1. Make the pickled chrysanthemum petals. Tear off the petals from the edible chrysanthemum flower plants. Bring the 400 ml of the water to a boil, add the 2 Tbs. of vinegar (not listed in the ingredients), and pour the petals. Keeping the petals on the bottom of the pan boil them for 1–2 minutes until the petals become soft over all. Pickle them in the sweetened vinegar from vinegar, sugar, and salt.

2. Add the plum vinegar in the freshly cooked rice and mix without kneading. Cool it down.

3. Cut the sea bream into slices at 7–8 mm/0.27–0.31 in. in size. Serve #2 in the dish, add #3, salmon roe, and chrysanthemum petals after draining its excess water.

Tofu Sushi in the Bowl

Simple and quick, *Tofu* sushi in the bowl is a casual menu with the good-matching combination of the *tofu* and sushi rice. The best way to go for it is to put fairly a lot of garnishes on and to pour a splash of the soy sauce. This recipe is also a perfect companion to the Japanese *sake*.

Ingredients (for 2 persons)

300 g/10.58 oz. silken *tofu*

2 pieces *myoga*

5–6 pieces flower of green perilla

30 g/1.05 oz. potherb mustard

1 Ts. black parched sesame

340 g/11.99 oz. sushi rice (see page 8)

1 Put the *tofu* in the bamboo basket and drain its excess water.

2 Finely chop the *myoga* and remove the stems from the flower of the green perilla. Cut the potherb mustard into pieces at 3 cm/1.18 in.

3 Serve the sushi rice in the dish, spread the potherb mustard on the rice. Roughly break #1 by hands and place it on the potherb mustard. Sprinkle the sesame, place the *myoga* and the flowers of the green perilla. Pour a splash of the soy sauce (not listed in the ingredients), to taste.

❖ Korean Seafood Sushi in the Bowl

Putting a lot of *sashimi* and fresh vegetables on the sushi rice, Korean seafood sushi in the bowl is full of volumes in its taste and look. It waters your mouth when putting the *gochujang*-based sauce over the dish. Eat it without mixing, Japanese style or mix the ingredients over all, in Korean style—Either one of them is at your discretion.

Ingredients (for 4 persons)

150 g/5.29 oz. natural yellowtail for *sashimi* (frozen fillet)

12 pieces sweet shrimp

1–2 pieces large leaf of red leaf lettuce

1 piece cucumber

1 bundle green sprout

Gochujang-based Sauce

2 Tbs. *gochujang*

1 Tbs. vinegar

2 Ts. soy sauce

1 Ts. sesame oil

1 Ts. sugar

Appropriate amount of toasted seaweed, cut into strips

1 Tbs. white parched sesame

680 g/23. 98 oz. sushi rice (see page 8)

a

b

1 Cut the yellowtail into thinner slices than the one when you eat as *sashimi* (see photo a). Remove the shells from the sweet shrimps, if any.

2 Tear the red leaf lettuce by hands in size for an easy bite. Chop off the roots from the green sprout.

3 Mix all the ingredients for the *gochujang*-based sauce (see photo b).

4 Serve the sushi rice in the bowls, put #1 and #2 on the top, and pour the sauce over all. Sprinkle the seaweed and sesame.

Sushi in the Bowl

❚❚ Western-style Sushi in the Bowl

The ingredients of this recipe are raw ham, paprika, half-dried tomato, olive fruits, and Parmesan cheese. The source of the savory is basil.

Such Italian combination goes well for the sushi rice with the Balsamic vinegar.

Topping anchovies prompts an aromatic savory on the dish.

a   b   c

Ingredients (for 4 persons)

40 g/1.41 oz. raw ham

30 g/1.05 oz. half-dried tomato

$1/2$ piece yellow paprika

8–9 pieces seedless black olive

5–6 pieces basil

20 g/0.70 oz. blocked Parmesan cheese

Sushi Rice

680 g/23.98 oz. freshly cooked rice

2 Tbs. balsamic vinegar

3 pieces anchovy

1 Tbs. minced parsley

1 Pour the half-dried tomato in hot water, leave it for approx. 10 minutes, and reconstitute the seasoning (see photo a). Dice it at 1.5 cm/0.59 in. in size.

2 Make sushi rice. Put the freshly cooked rice in the bowl, distribute the Balsamic vinegar evenly (see photo b), mix them together without kneading. Mince the anchovies and add it with the parsley (see photo c). Mix them together further.

3 Broil the paprika over the direct flame for 5–6 minutes until its skin is completely burned. Turn down the sides and cook further for 1–2 minutes. Once it is cooled down, peel the skin and cut them into strips at 7–8 mm/0.27–0.31 in.

4 Halve the black olive fruits, and tear the raw hams and basils with the hands. Scrape off the pieces of the Parmesan cheese using the peelers.

5 Add #1 and #3 on #2, leaving a little amount for each for the later decoration. Mix all together without kneading.

6 Serve #5 on the dish and scatter the rest of the seasonings and #4.

❖ Curry and Minced Meat Sushi in the Bowl

The curry and minced meat sushi in the bowl represents the Asian style in the sushi art, with the curry-flavored minced meat, the fried crunchy cloves of garlic, and nuts.

Ingredients (for 4 persons)

150 g/5.29 oz. beef ground with pork

2 chips garlic

1 Tbs. salad oil

1/2 Tbs. curry powder

1 Tbs. soy sauce

1 Tbs. sweetened *sake*

A sprinkling of salt

40 g/1.41 oz. mixed nuts

2 pieces large lettuce leaf

2 bundles coriander

680 g/23.98 oz. sushi rice (see page 8)

1 Cut the garlic into thin slices.

2 Pour the salad oil and garlic into the frying pan and put it over a fire with low flame. Deep-fry the garlic slowly in the oil until golden brown for 2–3 minutes. Once it gets crunchy, pick it up on the paper towel to dry.

3 Put the ground meat in the #2 frying pan and stir-fry it over the medium flame. Once the meat is flaked, add the curry powder, soy sauce, sweetened *sake*, and salt. Stir-fry further until it reduces the liquid.

4 Coarsely chop the mixed nuts and tear the lettuce leaves with hands for an easy bite. Cut the corianders into 2 cm/0.78 in. in length.

5 Serve the sushi on the plate, scatter the lettuce, and top #3 on the surface. Spread the mixed nuts and crunchy garlic and top the corianders.

▦ Orange Sushi in the Bowl

This salad-style sushi in the bowl highlights the trilogy of the aromatic tastes coming from the raw hams, oranges, and watercresses. By stuffing the ingredients in the scooped-out orange halves, it turns out to be an enjoyable hors d'oeuvre.

Ingredients (for 2 persons)

1 piece whole orange

40 g/1.41 oz. raw ham

$^1/_4$ piece purple onion

1 bundle watercress

Dressing

1 Tbs. olive oil

1 Tbs. white wine vinegar

1 Ts. whole grain mustard

$^1/_3$ Ts. salt

A sprinkling of pepper

340 g/11.99 oz. freshly cooked rice

1   Halve the whole orange, hollow out its flesh, and remove its seeds. Dice it at 7–8 mm/0.27–0.31 in. Keep the skins as we use them for the vessel at a later stage.

2   Cut the raw hams into pieces for an easy bite. Coarsely chop the purple onions. Pick up the leaves only of the watercress. If the leaves are too long, halve them.

3   Mix the ingredients for the dressing.

4   Put the rice in the bowl, distribute #3 evenly, mix without kneading. Add the orange fleshes, raw hams, purple onions, and watercress by leaving a little amount for the later decoration. Mix them together.

5   Serve the abundant amount of #4 on the orange skins, and top the rest of the watercress for decoration.

⬛ Steamed Sushi *Mushi Zushi*

You will realize the real charm of the steamed sushi when you cram the hot and steamy bite in your mouth, just after the cooked dishes pop out from the food steamer. You can use the left-over from the dinner table last night. Steaming both the food and dishes together is so handy to pass on the meal table. Use your imagination and add anything you want on the sushi rice, and you will be amazed at the broad selection of the ingredients you can choose.

Steamed Conger Eel Sushi, Osaka Style

Conger eel is the essential ingredient in the steamed sushi category,

and this recipe is famous for using the own ceramic ware per persons.

Other necessary items for this classic recipe are shrimps, eggs, snow peas,

and toasted seaweed as the source of the savory. The rule of the method is to use

as much different color variations of the ingredients as possible.

Once it is steamed, even the left-over sushi rice in the previous day is still delicious.

Ingredients (for 2 persons)

1 piece broiled conger eel

2 pieces shrimp in small size, without heads, with shells

3 thin omelet to make the julienned strips (see page 10)

4 pieces snow pea

Appropriate amount of toasted seaweed cut into strips

340 g/11.99 oz. sushi rice (see page 8)

1. Cut the conger eel into pieces at 2–3 cm/0.78–1.18 in.

2. Remove the digestive tracts and shells, except one joint of the tails from the shrimps. Boil the water in the pan, put the shrimps for 1 minute, and pick them up on the colander to drain the excess water. Remove the stems and from the snow peas.

3. Serve the sushi rice on the dish, scatter the seaweed, and distribute the julienned strips of the thin omelets. Layer the conger eels slightly at angles (see photo a) and add the shrimps and snow peas on the dish.

4. Put the dishes in the food steamer, cover the lid with the washcloth (see photo b), and steam the dishes for 3–4 minutes.

a

b

❖ Steamed Oyster Sushi, Simple Style

The steamed oyster retains the condensed aroma inside. This oyster sushi is such a recipe to taste it to a turn. The simplicity of the cooking method can apply to other shell meats, such as the scallops or clams.

Ingredients (for 2 persons)

300 g/ 10.58 oz. oyster

1 Tbs. fruits of Japanese pepper

2 Tbs. *sake*

1 Tbs. soy sauce

1 Tbs. sugar

20 g/0.70 oz. Japanese honewort

340 g/11.99 oz. such rice (see page 8)

1. Put the oyster and 1 Tbs. of the salt (not listed in the ingredients), gently wash them until the smudge is floating off. Repeat washing by changing the water for a few more times. Drain the water.

2. Pour #1, fruits of the Japanese pepper, *sake*, soy sauce, and sugar and put it over a fire. Boil down for 3–4 minutes until the liquid reduces completely and the body of the oyster is plumping. Turn off the heat.

3. Put the sushi rice in the heat-resistant containers (in the above example I am using the bamboo boxes), place the oysters on the surface, and distribute the

boiled liquid evenly on the sushi rice (see photo).

4. Put the containers in the food steamer, cover the lid with the washcloth, and steam them for 3–4 minutes. Cut the Japanese honewort into slices at 3 cm/1.18 in. and add them to the sushi dish as a decoration.

Steamed Sakura Shrimp and Edamame Sushi

To complete this sushi, you need to combine the two different techniques—pressing and steaming. First create the pressed sushi by mixing the boiled *hijiki* in the sushi rice, and apply the scrambled egg, *sakura* shrimps, *edamame* beans on top. Then cut into pieces and steam. The colors and ingredients in this sushi remind us that the spring has come.

Ingredients (for 2 persons. Use the mold at 18 x 10 x 5 cm/7.08 x 3.93 x 1.96 in.)

Boiled *hijiki*

5 g/0.17 oz. *hijiki*'s leaf

100 ml soup stock

1 Tbs. sweetened *sake*

1/2 Tbs. soy sauce

1 Ts. sugar

1/4 Ts. salt

1 piece egg to make the scrambled egg (see page 11)

10 g/0.35 oz. *sakura* shrimp

30 g/1.05 oz. boiled *edamame* bean (remove skins beforehand)

340 g/11.99 oz. such rice (see page 8)

2 pieces *hajikami* ginger (see page 17)

1. Make the boiled *hijiki* first. Reconstitute the *hijiki* leaves in the water and drain it in the colander. Pour the soup stock, sweetened *sake*, soy sauce, sugar, and salt, and put it over a fire. Add *hijiki* and boil down until you let the liquid reduce completely. Turn off the heat.

2. Squeeze #1 out to remove the excess water and mix it with the sushi rice (see photo a).

3. Place #2 in the mold and level the surface. Spread the scrambled eggs on it and scatter the *edamame* beans and *sakura* shrimps. Cover the surface with the cling film and press hard using the pressing lid. Remove the sushi from the mold and halve them.

4. Place #3 in the dish and put it in the food steamer (see photo b). Cover the lid with the washcloth, and steam them for 3–4 minutes. Cut the *hajikami* gingers into half and add in the dish for decoration.

Steamed Chicken and Mixed Vegetable Sushi

Steamed chicken and mixed vegetable sushi is the combination of the crispy broiled chicken and mushrooms, chestnuts, and vegetables in an assembled style. Press the ingredients in a small steaming bamboo basket per persons, and layer the baskets in the multiple deckers. Spread the bamboo leaves within the basket; it is easier to pull out the ready food. You can substitute the chicken to the *yakitori*, broiled chicken meat balls, or salmon.

Ingredients (for 2 persons)

Broiled Chicken

1 piece chicken breast meat

$^1/_2$ Tbs. soy sauce

$^1/_2$ Tbs. sweetened *sake*

50 g/1.76 oz. king trumpet mushroom

30 g/1.05 oz. *shimeji* mushroom

$^1/_8$ piece carrot

100 ml soup stock

$^1/_2$ Tbs. soy sauce

$^1/_2$ Tbs. sweetened *sake*

2–4 pieces candied chestnut

3–4 pieces boiled green vegetable (see page 14)

340 g/11.99 oz. sushi rice (see page 8)

1. Make the broiled chicken. Cut the chicken meat for an easy bite, add it in the bowl, and season it with the soy sauce and sweetened *sake*. Bring it for a grill with the medium flame. Spend 3–4 minutes per side (see photo a).

2. Cut the king trumpet mushrooms for an easy bite and cut further into the 6 portions equally. Split the *shimeji* mushrooms into a couple of batches. Cut the carrots into slices at 6 mm/0.23 in. and die cut to the maple shape.

3. Pour the soup stock, soy sauce, sweetened *sake* and bring it to a boil. Add #2 and cook on a low flame for 2–3 minutes. Then change the heat to the medium flame for 1–2 minutes until the liquid goes dry completely. Place the finished ingredients in the drainer.

4. Spread the bamboo leaves (not listed in the ingredients) in each of the steaming baskets. Place the sushi rice equally to each of the baskets, pile the half amount of #1, #3, and candied the chestnuts. Cut the green vegetables into 3 equal portions and add its halves to decorate.

5. Install the steaming baskets on the pot (see photo b). Close the lid and steam them for 3–4 minutes.

a

b

Steamed Vegetarian and Brown Rice Sushi

The secret of the deliciousness in this recipe is to use the brown rice for sushi rice, and deep-fried *tofu* to mix. Add a few varieties of the green vegetables, and lotus root to highlight its pure white color. The vegetables with the round sections give an adorable and delicious impression. Make this steamed sushi with the steaming basket at a larger size, and serve it with the basket on the table for everyone to share.

Ingredients (for 2 persons)

$^1/_3$ piece zucchini

2 pieces asparagus

4–5 pieces snap pea

30 g/1.05 oz. lotus root

30 g/1.05 oz. saltwort

100 ml soup stock

1 Tbs. light soy sauce

1 Tbs. sweetened *sake*

$^1/_3$ Ts. salt

1 piece deep-fried *tofu* (see page 82)

340 g/11.99 oz. freshly cooked brown rice

Rice Vinegar-based Sushi Dressing

2 Tbs. vinegar

$^1/_2$ Tbs. sugar

$^1/_4$ Ts. salt

1 Cut the zucchini into thin strips. Remove the hard cores of the roots in the asparagus and cut into diagonal slices at 4 cm/1.57 in. Eliminate the stems and strings of the snow peas and split them vertically into two halves.

Peel the skin of the lotus root and cut into thin slices.

2 Cut the saltwort roughly into strips.

3 Pour the soup stock, light soy sauce, sweetened *sake*, and salt in the pan. Bring them to a boil, add #1, cook them by turning down the top and bottom sides over the medium flame (see photo a) for 1 minute. Add #2, and mix the ingredients for 15 seconds. Drain the excess water in the colander.

4 Mix the ingredients of the rice

vinegar-based sushi dressing. Cut the deep-fried *tofu* into rectangular shapes at 5 mm/0.19 in.

5 Pour the brown rice into the bowl or rice-cooking tub, distribute the sushi dressing evenly (see photo b), mix them without kneading. Add the deep-fried *tofu* (see photo c). Mix them without kneading.

6 Place #5 in the food steamer, add #2 on top, and scatter the other vegetables. Close the lid, and steam the basket for 2 minutes. Make sure not to ruin the vegetable colors as the steaming time is too long.

◼ Soup Variations

Soup with Beaten Egg

Ingredients (for 2 persons)

1 egg beaten

400 ml soup stock

1 Ts. soy sauce

$^1/_3$ Ts. salt

Appropriate amount of powdered Japanese pepper

1. Pour the soup stock, soy sauce, and salt and bring them to a boil. Pour the beaten egg.
2. Once the egg floats and solidifies, turn off the heat.
3. Pour the appropriate amount into the soup bowls and sprinkle the Japanese powdered pepper.

Fried Burdock Soup

Ingredients (for 2 persons)

60 g/2.11 oz. burdock

2 pieces sliced bacon

$^1/_3$ Ts. salad oil

400 ml water

1 Ts. granular soup stock

$^1/_2$ Ts. soy sauce

$^1/_4$ Ts. salt

A sprinkle of coarsely ground black pepper

1. Shave off the skin of the burdock and cut it into long thin shaving. Cut the bacons into strips at 5 mm/0.19 in. at width.
2. Pour the salad oil in the heated frying pan, stir-fry #1, and add the water, granular soup stock, soy sauce, and salt listed in the ingredients. Bring them to a boil.
3. Pour the appropriate amount into the soup bowls and sprinkle the black pepper.

You may eat home-made sushi too much as it is so tasty. In such occasion, it is best to have a cup of the hot soup which make your stomach soothe. I have chosen the best combination of the ingredients to match particularly well to the sushi dishes here.

Natto Soup

Ingredients (for 2 persons)

40 g/1.41 oz. *natto*

$^1/_2$ pouch *nameko* mushroom

400 ml soup stock

2 Tbs. *miso*

2–3 pieces versatile leek finely chopped

1. Pour the soup stock in the pan and bring it to a boil. Add *natto* and *nameko* mushrooms and simmer them for approx. 1 minute.
2. Dissolve *miso* in the soup, add the versatile leek, and turn off the heat.

Miso Soup with Asari Clam and Tomato

Ingredients (for 2 persons)

150 g/5.29 oz. *asari* clam (remove the shell sand beforehand)

2 pieces large lettuce leaf

6 pieces cherry tomato

400 ml soup stock

$1^1/_2$ Tbs. *miso*

1. Wash the *asari* clams by scraping off the shells. Tear the lettuce leaves. Remove the stem of the cherry tomatoes and halve them.
2. Pour the soup stock in the pan, turn on the heat, and boil the *asari* clams.
3. Once the mouths of the clams are open, add the lettuce leaves and cherry tomatoes. Dissolve the *miso* immediately and turn off the heat.

⬛ Soup Alternatives

Steamed Egg Custard

Ingredients (for 2 persons)

Egg Liquid

1 piece egg

200 ml soup stock

1 Tbs. sweetened *sake*

$^1/_2$ Ts. soy sauce

$^1/_4$ Ts. salt

1 piece chicken breast strip

$^1/_3$ Ts. soy sauce

2 pieces *shiitake* mushroom (small, remove the stems)

4 pieces boiled shrimp

A sprinkling of sliced citron skin

Appropriate amount of Japanese honewort

1 Make the egg liquid first. Pour all the ingredients except the egg and bring them to a boil. Cool them down, mix with the egg, and filter the liquid.

2 Cut the chicken breast strip into at a 45-degree angle and marinate it with the soy sauce.

3 Put #2 in the heat-resistant dish and pour #1 after mixing (see photo).

4 Get the food steamer ready with full of spouting steams (or you can substitute it to the frying pan, using the washcloth. See page 117). Set #3 in the food steamer, close the lid, and steam for 1 minute over a medium to high flame. Open the lid, see if the surface of the custard

turns out to be white a little, turn the flame to low. Steam it for another 8–10 minutes to cook 80 % to the completion. Check carefully and frequently as a result varies according to the types of the steamers.

5 Add the *shiitake* mushrooms and shrimps on the surface, and steam for another 3 minutes until you can easily stick the chopstick into the mushrooms.

6 Add the sliced citron. skin and Japanese honewort on the top.

Everyone loves the steamed egg custard because it is so palatable and has a subtle flavor. It is an excellent companion to sushi dishes and can work as the alternative to the soup menu. Here are the two types—one for the standard, and the other with the harder egg custard.

Steamed and Dressed Egg Custard

Ingredients (for 4 persons)

Egg Liquid

2 pieces egg

300 ml soup stock

2 Tbs. sweetened *sake*

1 Ts. soy sauce

$^1/_3$ Ts. salt

60 g/2.11 oz. pork ground meat

50 g/1.76 oz. *shimeji* mushroom

$^1/_8$ piece each red and yellow paprika

$^1/_2$ piece cucumber

100 ml soup stock

1 Ts. soy sauce

1 Tbs. sweetened *sake*

$^1/_4$ Ts. salt

Starch Dispersed in Water

1 Ts. starch, 2 Ts. water

1　Make the egg liquid first. Pour all the ingredients except the egg and bring them to a boil. Cool them down, mix with the egg, and filter the liquid.

2　Lay washcloth on the bottom of the frying pan, pour the water in the middle of the pan's height and place the heat-hesitance dish on the washcloth. Pour #1 in the container (or use the food steamer instead. See page 116). Close the lid, and steam for 1 minute over a medium to high flame. Open the lid, see if the surface of the custard turns out to be white a little, turn the flame to low. Steam it for another 12–15 minutes. Check carefully and frequently as a result varies according to the types of the steamers.

3　Flake the *shimeji* mushrooms and halve them. Dice the paprika into 7–8 mm/0.27–0.31 in. in size, and cucumber into 1 cm/0.39 in. after peeling off the surface skins.

4　Pour the soup stock, soy sauce, sweetened *sake*, salt, and ground meat, and put them over the fire. Cook them while flaking the ground meat with the medium flame. Skim off the scum, add #3, and cook further for 1 more minute with the low flame. Prepare for the starch dispersed in water and dress it over #2.

Chinese Cabbage Leaves and Salted Kelp, Marinated with Lemon

Ingredients (for 2 persons)

200 g/7.05 oz. Chinese cabbage

2 pieces lemon cut into rings

10 g/0.35 oz. salted kelp

1 Ts. sesame oil

A sprinkling of salt

1   Tear the Chinese cabbage into pieces for an easy bite. Roughly chop the lemon.

2   Put #1 in the bowl and marinate it with salted kelp, sesame oil, and salt.

Radish Marinated with Spicy Cod Roe Mayo

Ingredients (for 2 persons)

200 g/7.05 oz. radish

30 g/1.05 oz. spicy cod roe

2 Tbs. mayonnaise

$1/2$ Ts. vinegar

1   Pare the radish in the ribbon shape, pour it into the bowl, and coat it with the $1/4$ Ts. of salt (not listed in the ingredients). Leave it for approx. 10 minutes and squeeze the excess water out.

2   Cut the spicy cod roe into strips at 5 mm/0.19 in. in width, put it in the bowl, and marinate it with the mayonnaise and vinegar.

3   Add #1 to #2 and marinate them lightly.

The principal ingredients of the sushi dishes are seafood and *sashimi* which tends to have a short of vegetables. Let's prepare for some intermezzo vegetable dishes to take a nutritional balance in your meals. Here I am introducing a few variations of the quick and easy vegetable dishes.

Spinach and Flaked Egg, Marinated with Sesame

Ingredients (for 2 persons)

200 g/7.05 oz. spinach

2 pieces egg to make the flaked egg (see page 11)

2 Tbs. black ground sesame

1 Tbs. soy sauce

1 Ts. sugar

1 Boil the spinach in hot water with a sprinkling of salt and drain its water in the colander. Cut it into strips at 3 cm/1.18 in. and squeeze the excess water.

2 Put the sesame oil, soy sauce, and sugar in the bowl and mix them. Add #1 and marinate them. Pour the flaked egg and marinate them lightly.

Carrot and Small Fish, Cooked with Salt

Ingredients (for 2 persons)

1 piece carrot   1 Tbs. sweetened *sake*

15 g/0.52 oz. small fish (*jako*)   1/4 Ts. salt

1 Ts. sesame oil

1 Cut the carrot into the rectangular slices at 3 cm/1.18 in. in size.

2 Add the sesame water to the heated frying pan, put #1, and stir-fry it over the medium flame for approx. 1 minute. Add the small fish and stir-fry further for 1–2 minutes.

3 When the small fishes are crunchy, season it with the sweetened *sake* and salt.

Let's Try Hand-shaped Sushi

The technique of the hand-shaped sushi is the legacy from the predecessor masters handing down to the posterity sushi chefs over the generations. Its skill is not something you can instantly achieve, but you may want to learn its ABC casually. In this page, I am showing how to make and eat the hand-shaped sushi. The key is to blow the air in the rice grains in the sushi rice, not holding the rice balls too tightly.

▪ Hand-shaped Sushi *Nigiri Zushi*

1
Sprinkle the vinegar water lightly on your both palms. Scoop the appropriate amount of sushi rice with your right palm, and organize the shape of sushi rice ball loosely.

2
Place the ingredient (lean tuna in this example) on the left palm and apply the grated wasabi on its surface.

3
Put the sushi ball on the ingredient as above.

4
Push the center area of the sushi ball a little with your left thumb, so that the air goes it through.

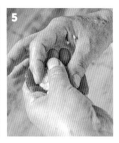
5
Hold the top and bottom of the sushi balls lightly with the right thumb and the index finger.

6
Place the right index and middle fingers on the sushi rice ball.

7
Stay both fingers on the sushi ball and hand-shape it.

8
Roll down the sushi ball upside down using your left thumb to the far end.

9
Hold the top of the ingredient with your left thumb, and the left and rights sides of the sushi with your right thumb and index finger to organize the shape of the sushi.

10
Hold down the sushi rice lightly with your right index and middle fingers, and the top of the sushi with your left thumb.

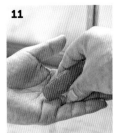
11
Rotate the direction of the sushi at 180 degrees.

12
Repeat #10 and #11 to organize the shape of sushi at all directions.

13
Hand-shaped sushi is complete. It is important to hand-shape quickly without spending too much time.

▪▪ Warship Sushi *Gunkan Zushi*

1

Sprinkle the vinegar water lightly on your both palms. Scoop a little more amount of sushi rice than the one for the hand-shaped sushi with your right palm, and organize the shape of sushi rice ball loosely.

2

Push the center area of the sushi ball a little with your left thumb, so that the air goes it through.

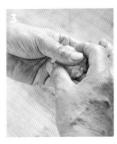

3

Hold the top and bottom of the sushi balls lightly with the right thumb and the index finger.

4

Roll the sushi ball to the far side and turn it upside down as above.

5

Hold down the sushi rice lightly with your right index and middle fingers, and the top of the sushi with your left thumb.

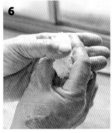

6

Use your right thumb and index fingers, left thumb to organize the same of the rice ball, just like you did for the hand-shaped roll.

7

Cut the toasted seaweed wider than the width of the sushi rice ball and run it around the sushi rice ball.

8

Warship roll is almost ready. The rest part is just to put the topping ingredients on.

9

Top the ingredient (salmon roe in this example) on the sushi rice to the top edge of the seaweed frame.

10

Warship roll is complete. You can apply this method to other ingredients.

Table Manner at the Sushi Restaurant

1. Eat without consuming too much time after serving

When the sushi is ready and placed in front of you, eat it without consuming too much time. Leaving the finished sushi without touching ruins the taste of sushi as its surface is beginning to dry. Both seaweed roll and the warship roll should be eaten before the seaweed gets wilted.

2. Have a general understanding of eating

Generally speaking, you should start from the white meat fish or other ingredients in the light taste, or shell meat that has not much fat. The fish meat with a lot of fat or the sushi whose surface gets the sweet sauce (such as the one for the conger eel) should eat later. This rule of the order is not absolute though.

3. Either chopsticks or hands are OK

Hand-shaped sushi was originally supposed to eat without using chopsticks, and the tradition remains valid. Using hands only for hand-shaped sushi is said to be more discreet. Sushi restaurant usually offers the damp towel before the meal starts to remove sushi rice sticking to your hands or the soy sauce stains, so you can simply wipe them off. If you have a hesitation to use your hands, going with the chopsticks has no problem as well.

4. Learn how to put soy sauce on your sushi

Pour a small amount of soy sauce on the small sauce plate first. Add more of it time to time.

a. Tilt the sushi horizontally and hold, put the ingredient part only on the soy source. Do not put the soy sauce on the sushi rice.

b. Hold the sushi with one hand, turn the ingredient upside down, and dip the ingredient only in the soy sauce.

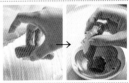

c. When you use the chopsticks, go with #a. Tilt the sushi horizontally and hold, and put the soy sauce only on the ingredient.

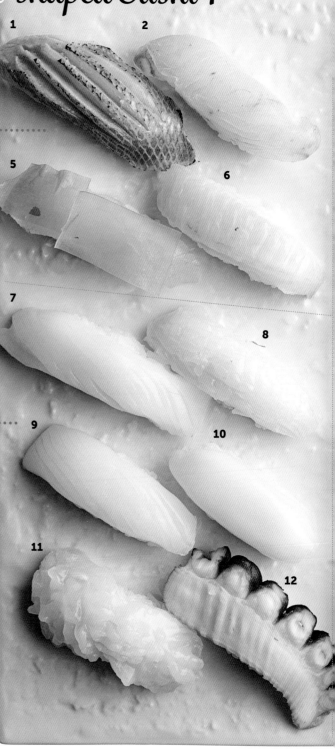

White Meat

1. Red Bream:
Broil the skin and bring out the fragrance.

2. Flat Fish: Eat raw.
Otherwise, it is tasty to press with the kelp.

3. Natural Yellowtail:
Yellowtail is called by different names as they grow larger. The young yellowtail is *inada*, middle-sized one is *warasa*, and they finally settle as matured yellowtail, *buri*.

4. Young Sea Bream: *Kasugo*.
Pickle the flesh lightly with vinegar.

5. Pickled Cod with Kelp: Arrange this recipe while the meat is still fresh.

6. Flounder Edge of Flat Fish: *Engawa*.
This refers to the muscle area to move the fin.

Calamari and Octopus

7. Kisslip Cuttlefish:
Its flesh is usually thick and tender, gaining best popularity among all calamari.

8. Swordtip Squid:
This calamari has the short tip like the sword and is richly available in *Tottori* area.

9. Oval Squid: This squid is the king of the same species in its texture, taste, and scent.

10. Cuttlefish:
The taste is best when you sprinkle the salt over the flesh and eat without soy sauce.

11. North Pacific Giant Octopus:
Make cross-hatching cuts in the body before using as the ingredients.

12. Common Octopus (raw):
The photo on the right shows the leg parts of the boiled flesh.

Silver-skinned Fish (Bluefin)

13. Pickled Gizzard Shad:
Use its middle size. Arrange pickles while the flesh is still fresh.

14. *Shinko*: This is the name given to the young gizzard shad and is available only between the mid-July and August.

15. Pickled Mackerel:
The roasted style is popular as well.

16. Horse Mackerel: Eat with grated ginger or finely chopped spring onion.

17. Sardin: Eat with grated ginger or finely chopped spring onion.

18. Pacific Saury: Eat with grated ginger or finely chopped spring onion.

Shrimps, Prawns and Mantis Shrimp

19. Japanese Tiger Prawn:
Boil the raw flesh and enjoy the colors, scents, and sweetness.

20. Sweet Shrimp:
Use the raw flesh (usually 2 pieces) topping on the hand-shaped sushi.

21. *Botan* Shrimp:
Use the raw flesh and enjoy its sweetness.

22. Mantis Shrimp:
Boil the entire body with the shell. Apply the sweet sauce (*tsume*) on the surface.

Tuna

1. Lean Tuna Marinated in Soy Sauce (zuke): Use the soy sauce evaporated with *sake* or sweet *sake*.

2. Lean Tuna: Enjoy the authentic and natural deliciousness of the tuna meat.

3. Medium Fatty Tuna: Half lean and half fat, it contains the pure sweetness.

4. Fattest Tuna: The marbled meat is in pale pink with white fat.

5. Broiled Tuna Collar: Use the marbled meat.

Roes and Crabs

6. Herring Roe: Use seaweed to wrap around.

7. Snow Crab: Its brand name is *Echizen* crab.

8. Sea Urchin: The example shown on the right is Anthocidaris, landed on *Rebun* Island, the furthest north part of *Hokkaido*.

9. Salmon Roe: Marinated in soy sauce.

10. Salted Salmon Roe: Marinated in salt usually keeps the fresh color. Perfect for the warship roll.

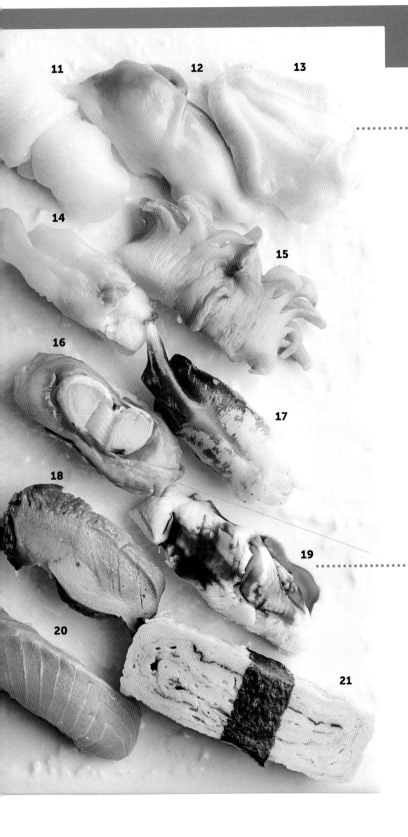

12 13 14 15 16 17 18 19 20 21

Shellmeat

11. Scallop:
Pictured on the left is the adductor of the scallop, good for boiling or broiling.

12. Sakhalin Surf Clam:
The characteristic of this clam is the bright purple with gradation.

13. Japanese Ivory Shell: Cut the shell meat into silvers to prepare the ingredients.

14. Chinese Mactra: Prepare for the adductor muscle for the warship roll.

15. Bloody Clam:
Knock the meat down on the cutting board to tighten the shell meat.

16. Bloody Clam Mantle: Mantle contains the full flavors of the ocean.

17. Heart Clam: Use the flesh meat or steam it to hand-roll.

Others

18. Boiled Abalone: The photograph on the left is the shell meat to boil until it is tender. Boiled abalone is known as one of the most expensive sushi ingredients.

19. Roasted Conger Eel: Broil and enjoy the eel's roasted aroma. Apply the sweet sauce on the surface. Tasting simply with the salt only is delicious too.

20 Raw Salmon: Raw or broiled, it is one of the most popular ingredients.

21. Thick Egg Rolls with Seaweed:
Roll the thick egg rolls with the seaweed, being aware of a little bit of more sugar to add.

The Art of Rolled Sushi

The essential ingredients for the rolled sushi
are sushi rice and seaweed.
Its finished size is approximately 10 cm/3.93 in.
in diameter and 12 cm/4.72 in. and weight at
1,160 g/40.91 oz.

Ukiyo-e Beauty

Hair: black sesame and powdered red perilla
Mouth: paprika
Background: cod fish seasoned and flaked

"Hoping to create something no one has ever
looked at, I work on the sushi roll with no
rehearsal no matter how the pattern of the roll
is complicated", says **Tama-chan**, the sushi roll
artist. She started her career as the sushi roll
artist in 2005, naming her artworks as
"Smiling Sushi Roll" with slogan of
"Smile when making, smile when looking at,
and smile when eating".
The ingredients of her sushi rolls consist of
something familiar to the Japanese people,
yet the scenes illustrated on the surface of her
rolls are exceptional and full of surprises. If
you want to learn more about her artworks,
you may locate her book *Smiling Sushi Roll*.
(ISBN9784898153844)

Shibaraku in Kabuki

Eyes: pokeweed
Kabuki **makeup:** cod fish seasoned and flaked, red food coloring
Mouth and hair: seaweed and gourds
Part: cheese
Background: curry powder
(*Shibaraku* is one of the most popular programs in *Kabuki* performance.)

126

Sushi rolls, representing a very Japanese recipe, tell us who we are and where we originally stand.

The icons, such as *Ukiyo-e*, *Kabuki*, or *Kanji* are now globally universal as the symbol of Japan. These keywords also represent the *Edo* period, when the Japanese enjoy the blessings of peach and high culture.

Tama-chan shifts the position of the ingredients even in a piece of sushi roll. You will be amazed to see the different pictures every time you cut the rolls into pieces.

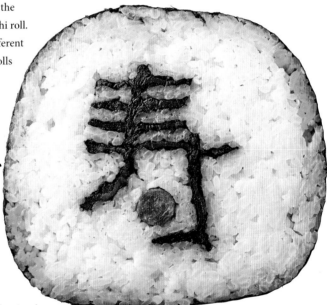

Kotobuki
(Japanese letter to represent the meaning of happiness)

Letter: seafood and gourd
Dot within the letter (represents the "sun" as well): salami
Border frame: pickled green perilla seeds, curry powder, cod fish seasoned and flaked, red food coloring, and sesame

Hatsue Shigenobu

Graduated from the Culinary Course at Hattori Nutrition College, **Hatsue** worked as the assistant at Oda Cooking College and to a food researcher. She then chose the position of the independent professional.

As an almighty cooking talent she takes over from the traditional and standard home cooking menu to the unusual and exotic recipes, she learned during her trips to overseas. She frequently appears on TV and writes for many food magazines, and authors a multiple number of cooking books.

Book Design: Takayuki Mogi

Photographer: Akio Takeuchi

Stylist: Kyoko Hijioka

Commissioning Editor: Kyoko Matsuhara

Sushi Roll Art: Tama-chan

Editor: Kaori Mori (Asahi Shimbun Publications Inc.)

English translation: Rico Komanoya

English proofreading: Aki Ueda (Pont Cerise)

Thanks to MORI ZUSHI for help with the photographing (pages 120–125)

4-1-30 Asahi-cho Akishima-shi Tokyo, 196-0025, JAPAN
TEL: +81 42 541 2840

Established in 1963, MORI ZUSHI is the well-known sushi restaurant to carry the natural ingredients only through their skillful cooking expertise. They are the favorite restaurant fully booked at all times.

Make Sushi at Home: Delicious and Easy Recipes for All Occasions
by Hatsue Shigenobu

Published in 2017 by:
NIPPAN IPS Co., Ltd.
1-3-4, Yushima
Bunkyo-ku, Tokyo, 113-0034

ISBN 978-4-86505-101-8

SUSHI COOK BOOK SUSHI RECIPE
© 2016 Asahi Shimbun Publications Inc.
First published in Japan in 2016 by Asahi Shimbun Publications Inc.

Publisher of Japanese Edition: Tsuyoshi Tsuda

Printed in China